"If you love Me, keep My commands.

And I will ask the Father,

and He will give you another Advocate

to help you and be with you forever –

the Spirit of truth. "

John 14:15-17

INTRODUCTION

The topic of spirituality has always been of great interest to many people. The new age offers a variety of countless directions for spiritual seekers, satisfying any taste and inclination. They are all claiming to possess true knowledge for spiritual ascension and freedom and salvation from life misfortunes and health ailments. Gurus, spiritual teachers, prophets, priests, faith-healers, energy-healers, etc., are emerging from all sides, trying to warn, to predict, to enlighten, to heal, to guide… "But the seekers' cry for light, imbued with strengths to cleave through the mire, is turned aside and dies away beneath an impenetrable canopy, assiduously set up by the very people who think they help. *They offer stones for bread!*" (Abd-Ru-Shin, *In the Light of Truth*).

Notice the pouring amount of literature on the topic of spirituality or so-called psychic science suddenly appearing, bombarding, and overwhelming the genuine seekers for Light. It does not animate but only exhausts the human spirit! With that, the authors prove the fruitlessness of all they offer, for whatever drains the spirit is never right. Still, many people appoint themselves to different religious teachings and spiritual practices, thinking they will be delivered to a new height. But, at the very least, all they will eventually encounter is a great disappointment. For none of those gurus offer the real deal. The world we live in is proof of that.

If one tries to objectively examine the present situation, they will see that modern humanity claims to possess spiritual values while increasingly spiraling down the path of lies, violence, and debauchery. The reason for that is quite clear. However, there is no serious attempt to resolve the issue. Is there a single person who doesn't have at least one of the following vices: envy, greed, vanity, anger, irritability, resentment, sadness, fear, lust, the list goes on? From a religious point of view, these are all sins for which each of us is held accountable. Whether we acknowledge the Laws of the Creator or not, it does not change in any way their unshakable effect on our lives. Ignorance is not an excuse from responsibility. So, sinful people form families, communities, nations, and, eventually, all of humanity. We live outside of the Law of creation, and we suffer accordingly. That is the highest form of justice.

Nevertheless, despite the apparent global decline in the overall moral health of humanity, people refuse to stop in their tracks and re-assess the validity of the path they have been heading. With that, they are throwing away perhaps the very last chance to escape the fate of the one caught in the quicksand. "He who makes no effort to grasp the word of the Lord aright burdens himself with guilt!" (Abd-Ru-Shin). Possibly for the last time, man is offered to either walk towards God or to remain in the arms of his demons. *"There is a judge for the one who rejects Me and does not accept My words; the very words I have spoken will condemn them at the last day."* (John, 12:48).

Bibliografische Information der Deutschen Nationalbibliothek: Die Deutsche Nationalbibliothek verzeichnet diese Publikation in der Deutschen Nationalbibliografie; detaillierte bibliografische Daten sind im Internet über dnb.dnb.de abrufbar.
Bibliographic information from the German National Library: The German National Library lists this publication in the German National Bibliography; detailed bibliographic data can be called up on the Internet at dnb.dnb.de.

Herstellung und Verlag: BoD – Books on Demand, Norderstedt
Production and publishing: BoD – Books on Demand, Norderstedt

ISBN: 9783751997355

GEORGE RAY

THE TIME
IS NOW

1. PURPOSE OF HUMAN LIFE

When talking about spirituality, we must start with the concept of spirit. So, let's try to understand just what a spirit is. A human being is not only a physical body but also a sum of fields. As humans, we have the ability to think and feel, displaying a wide range of emotions that have a significant impact on our mood. So, what influences our mood, good or bad? Often, we may not be in physical pain, but our mood is down, which means our field is distorted. Waves of harmony cover us when we feel good, which we tend to distort due to our misplaced reactions to various life events. These are the negative reactions we have towards our family relationships, between men and women, parents and children, or even to our government. This upsets us, causing us to lose balance; as a result, our mood deteriorates. We are faced daily with undesirable moments, and the negativity involuntarily appears in our lives. So, let's discuss ways to avoid and resist this negativity. But first, we need a foundation. We need to understand exactly what a human is and on what basis we can fight off the negativity.

Unfortunately, the doctrine of materialism is practically run dry. The world arranged by materialists is coming to an end. We cannot live in this world without a soul, but a human soul has its own physics. Let's refer to Infinity (Illustration 1). Call it Universal Consciousness, the Creator, or God; the terminology makes no difference. Below It, there is a multilayered Creation: Primordial Spiritual Creation (the World of Primordial Beings), Secondary Spiritual Creation (the Spiritual World) consisting of Conscious Spiritual World and Unconscious Spiritual World, the Sphere of Animistic Substantiality, the Ethereal World, the Astral World, and the World of Matter (the World of Manifested Matter or Physical World). The Physical World consists of electrons, protons, and neutrons arranged in atoms. Atoms join to form molecules, which in turn compose tissue. Nature encompasses minerals, organic matter in the form of plants and animals, and, finally, a human. What relates us to nature, such as minerals, plants, and animals? We are all made of electrons, protons, and neutrons composed in chemical chains. But what makes us, humans, different as a form of life?

Creation has a certain hierarchy (Illustration 1). Here on Earth, besides minerals, plants, animals, and humans, we also have such elements of nature as fire, water, and air. This was all created through an intermediary.

CREATOR

= INFINITY = GOD = HOLY FATHER IN HEAVEN

LIGHT

(HOLY SPIRIT =WILL OF GOD)

Primordial Spiritual
●----------Creation

HUMAN
SPIRIT

Secondary Spiritual
●----------Creation

CONSCIOUS

UNCONSCIOUS

ACTUATING MECHANISM
OF THE UNIVERSE

Sphere of Animistic
●----Substantiality

●--Ethereal World

●-----Astral World

Humans
Animals
Plants
Minerals
Elements (Fire,
Water, Earth, Air)

●-------------World
of Matter
(Physical World)

Ill.1

CREATOR

REVELATION

REAL CONNECTION WITH GOD

Primordial Spiritual
Creation ----------

CONSCIOUS

UNCONSCIOUS

SPIRIT

Secondary Spiritual
Creation ----------

SPIRITUAL SEEDS

Sphere of Animistic
Substantiality ---

CLOAK OF
ANIMISTIC
SUBSTANTIALITY

Ethereal World -

ETHEREAL
CLOAK

Astral World ---

ASTRAL
CLOAK

World of Matter
(Physical ----------
World)

MATERIAL
CLOAK

Ill.2

This intermediary is an actuating mechanism of the Universe or forces that originate from a layer of the Creation called Animistic Substantiality. Our ancestors used to worship these forces, calling them "gods". It was a practice of polytheism or paganism. Later, the human spirit grew to understand that there is only one Creator. God *never imposes* this concept on any of us! God is consciously and patiently waiting for us to *voluntarily* come to faith because He has granted us freedom of choice.

A human is a creature born in the Spiritual Sphere of the Secondary Creation (Illustration 1). We resemble a lens born by Light. In religious terms, this Light is the Holy Spirit or the Will of God. In prayers, we call God "our Holy Father in Heaven". God does not dwell within the bounds of His Creation. He never enters it, but His Will does. God's Will permeated His Creation and established Laws *which we must learn, respect, and live by if we want to find joy.* For we ourselves were born by these Laws. There are several fundamental Laws of the Creation, such as the Law of Retribution (the Law of Justice), the Law of Freedom of Choice, the Law of Resemblance, the Law of Motion, the Law of Evolution, the Law of Attraction, and the Law of Separation.

The Holy Spirit, the Will of God, created a human spirit and taught this creature to communicate with Him. This form of communication is called "revelation". It is described in the Bible as a revelation of saints - the real connection with God taking the forms of images and intuitive perceptions. One day this creature, the human spirit, will have to transform from the unconscious to a conscious human being. In other words, the small structure of Light must discover and understand this world, thus transforming itself into a conscious state of being. *That is the very purpose of human life in general terms.* How do we achieve this transformation? In our base form, we resemble weak seeds that have been planted into soil (Illustration 2). We cannot ascend to the Conscious Spiritual World from our initial point as we are too weak, inert, and ignorant. To gain strength and knowledge, we must learn about the Creation through personal experience. Thus, we have been given an opportunity to descend into much denser worlds, acquiring "cloaks" to act as covers, allowing us to partake in the lives of these worlds. Similarly, many years ago when we descended to Earth, we received the physical body of the ape. Eventually, we began our transformation into homo-sapiens, acting under the pressure of our spiritual will.

Within the concept of spirit, or human *"I"*, is embedded creativity and the ability to love. Where did all of this come from? From God! God is Love, and God is the Creator! So, He endowed His children with the ability to love, to create beauty, and to sacrifice in the name of interests far more significant than their own. Animals are incapable of this. Animals come from the Animistic Substantiality, another Sphere of the Creation, and have never been human. Likewise, humans have never been animals. But humans use the cloak of the animistic substantiality, of the animal, to gain presence in the Physical World.

About 4.5-5 billion years ago, wrapped in several delicate cloaks called *"soul"*, the human spirit descended from the Spiritual Sphere and invaded the body of the ape - the most advanced species in the animal kingdom. From that moment, the human creature began to walk the Earth. This creature wore the material cloak and was simultaneously under the pressure of the Light – *"learn to live!"* As soon as we learn to live righteously on Earth, we will ascend to the Ethereal World, then to the Sphere of Animistic Substantiality and, finally, back to our origin – the Spiritual World. That is our trajectory as spiritual creatures. We undertake the journey from the unconscious to the conscious state, exploring all of these worlds through personal experience (Illustration 2). Living righteously means learning the Laws of our Creator and *voluntarily submitting to Them using our will.*

2. THE FALL OF MAN

After the human came to Earth, hundreds of millions of years passed before he fell into sin. Unfortunately, the Fall of Man has not been sufficiently explained as a concept by either the Church, any religious cults, or esoteric groups. Attempts have been made, but in order to understand this theory, one must first and foremost learn to live by the Commandments. That is the only chance to come to revelation and to acquire reliable information to guide us. The one who does not live by the Commandments will never attain dependable information. Thus, he will always be misled.

There are certain forces of Darkness that exploit our laziness, or rather rely on it, in order to impart us with *false* information. We must recognize the concept of "Lucifer" or "Satan". The word "Satan" translates from ancient Hebrew as "the enemy", signifying the enemy of God. However, it is impossible to oppose God. It is impossible to go against the Will of God because Lucifer is also a creation of God. He is a former archangel. Lucifer has only the ability to challenge people, which he has succeeded at with great skill. As a result, we succumb to drowning in a swamp of sin due to our own laziness and foolishness.

So, what is a sin?

The human creature has an opportunity to create good or not to create good, which means we have the right to err. This is our freedom of choice! We are free to choose the path of evil, greed, or some other sin, where sin is a deviation from the norm of Law. The norm of Law is the flow of Light that descends from God, and any deviation from it is considered a sin. Worlds were created by the pressure of the Lines of Force, the Will of God, and we cannot oppose It! Moreover, we are also Light by birth, and our spirit is never mistaken. Unfortunately, we allowed ourselves to become ensnared by the Darkness through our "voice of reason" and through our own feelings, ignoring the spirit. We made our rational mind (the tool of logic) the chief commander, putting our conscience aside; thus, we voluntarily closed ourselves off from our soul, our spirit. As a result, we live, think, and feel erroneously. We experience incorrect reactions to this world, thus drowning deeper and deeper, and we are well aware of it. It is quite evident that despite living in the day and age of advanced science, education, and highly developed intellectual skills, humanity is spiraling down the path of destruction.

In search of an explanation for this tragic phenomenon, people have proposed a number of theories that come very close to being accurate. In reality, being "very close" isn't close enough – *not exact!* Satan uses this trick by giving 95-99% of the correct information. However, the rest is *false* and always surrounding key issues, *especially* when it comes to the Connection between man and God! That is how, through Satan, the concept of materialism was born, *which is the renouncement of our Higher Connection.* Consequently, man has been left within the grasp of physical matter, *believing there is nothing else.* But there are still a few people who believe in the *real* truth – that there is so much more.

Satan built his first fort called "materialism", but people with a deeper sense are trying to search beyond it. The Bible calls them the searching ones: "Seek and you will find" (Matthew, 7:7). Those who seek beyond physical matter come across another route, offered in the form of religious cults and esoteric groups. Jesus warned us, "...and many false prophets will appear and deceive many people" (Matthew, 24:11), "false messiahs and false prophets will appear and perform great signs and wonders to deceive, if possible, even the elect." (Matthew, 24:24). This is the essence of all cults and occult practices. *They do not offer a breakthrough to the Light.* The breakthrough happened when I learned to live by the Commandments, which is the Law of God!

To live by the Law means not only submitting to It with our thoughts, which do not extend beyond the Physical World. Thoughts, words, and deeds are three domains of our being that pertain solely to the Physical World. *But the human being encompasses so much more than that!*

Following the world of gross matter, the realm of our feelings begins. In parapsychology, they call it the Astral World. If our physical matter and our thought processes carry the speed of electromagnetic waves (C = 300,000 km/sec), then the realm of our feelings operates at a far greater speed - about 400C. This speed was once available, to some degree, only to the secret services. All materials were classified. The speed eventually became accessible to scientists studying torsion physics - the physics of fast waves. Now, there is a technology that has been researched and applied in this field.

A man consists not only of deeds, words, thoughts, and feelings, but also of *higher limits* called the soul. However, our souls are blocked from us. The human soul operates with the speed of waves much higher than

400C, but those waves become available to us only on one condition – that we live by the Commandments. Jesus Christ once said, "No one comes to the Father except through Me" (John 14:6). What exactly does this mean? To help you gain a better understanding, I will be applying both religion and physics.

Who was Jesus as a phenomenon? God issued a unit of Light, and part of the Creator came to Earth. The whole of God can never descend to Earth because Creation is a finite value. Hence the term "space and time". This term speaks of *limited value*, something *created*, whereas God is *infinite* by definition! Thus, the Infinity cannot invade the finite, or else He will destroy it, burst it. This concept is elementary. But the part of the Infinity that was necessary to persuade people not to commit evil has come. However, Jesus *could not force* people to reform. He could only *offer* it because of our freedom of choice!

3. REDEMPTION THROUGH FORGIVENESS

By the Law of Freedom of Choice, one of the fundamental Laws of the Creation, a man can choose to do bad or good. If he does good, then by the Law of Retribution or "what you sow, so must you reap a hundredfold" (the reciprocal action or cause-and-effect), he receives great fortune, health, and prosperity in return. If he does wrong and makes mistakes, he receives misfortune. Sinning is the root of all problems, including trouble in your personal life and bad health. This is an automatic system - what you sow, that must you reap a *hundredfold*. Think of sowing a seed of wheat and in return, you harvest an ear of grain containing many seeds. And if you plant a seed of an invasive species, that unwanted weed will sprout and take over your entire yard! Similarly, if there is a person who is mostly acting right, but still has even minor deviations from the norm, he will inevitably experience misfortunes.

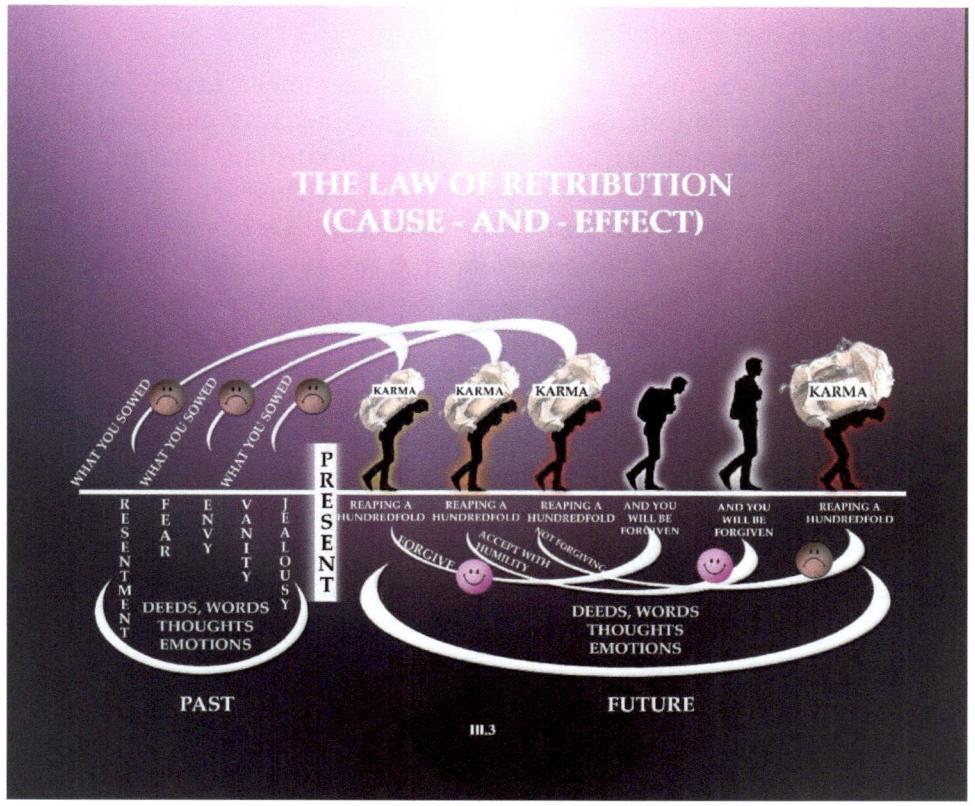

Let's draw a straight line representing an individual's personal life and mark it with today's date (Illustration 3). How many people can say they were saints in the past? Probably none. Thus, unless one is holy, then he has some deviations from being right *and not only in his deeds*. Suppose he is almost always acting right, and he is a decent person. But he can be rude at times, perhaps occasionally uttering an offensive word. Furthermore, he has some thoughts that he does not voice. He can think poorly of someone, even when it seems an accurate appraisal. However, he thinks bad thoughts without realizing the other developments that come into play. While thinking a negative thought, he might get emotional, feeling annoyed, offended, jealous, or conceited, depending on the nature of the thought. He might feel the need to brag a little, to embellish the truth, or to present himself as a better person than he really is, perhaps to benefit his business. Has this not been the case for many? Perhaps not entirely, but certainly to some extent. All these emotions, thoughts, words, and sometimes deeds create our past. And we are held accountable for each and every one of them, ***including our emotions***!

Practically everyone experiences vanity, resentment, irritability, fears, and jealousy. I won't mention the full range of negative emotions. There are villains, those who are cruel and downright horrible. But let's instead focus only on the most ordinary people who have these five negative qualities I have just listed. So, the average person reaps a *hundredfold* of that he has sown; meaning, ***the punishment is always far greater than the crime committed***. That is the pedagogical reception of God, and there is nothing we can do about it, for He created the worlds! So, there will come a time when we receive some heavy load of misfortunes. Suppose we are robbed, or not given our fair share, or we are failing in our career, or we are treated unethically, or we do not have peace at home, or any manner of adversities. There are many scenarios of disadvantageous life circumstances. All of that is the result of our past. Every one of us has sowed it, and now we are all reaping it. Now, summarize this and project it onto the entire nation: all the Jones', the Smiths, the Andersons, the Wilsons, and others - what they sow, that they reap, and reap, and reap.

To end this perpetual and seemingly impossible battle against life misfortunes, one must first abolish their negative emotions. And it's quite difficult to do. Why so? Go ahead and try to live without fear and reproach. I, too, once had to face this challenge. It seemed impossible for me to accomplish! How can one eliminate fear? How can one get rid of resentment?

Vanity seemed easier to abolish. I just had to stop instances of bragging. But what about the feeling of being offended? It seems that if someone is insulting me, then I'm the victim and I have a right to feel offended! Let's take a closer look.

Presume I was robbed, and I became upset and angry. I am the victim in the here and now. However, I must remind myself that perhaps I have done some harm to an individual in the past. And that loss for someone in the past led to a huge loss for me today. That is, we cannot consider justice in the context of *only one day.* It must be viewed in the context of our entire lifetime. And sometimes, not just one lifetime. I *must* lose by the Law of Retribution, and I must accept it as fair. If I accept it as fair, I show *humility.* Then God says, "You amended your mistake by redeeming it with your suffering. Thus, you are no longer guilty in this particular instance." That is how it happens every time. If you consider accepting and applying this principle in your daily life, the battle against your sins begins.

At first, it is hard to accept all misfortunes with humility because we have enormous inertia. We continue to react wrongly, as we have always done. It is impossible to become righteous immediately. It takes many years to accomplish. But the one who is willing keeps working, and the one who is not willing doesn't work, grounded in their freedom of choice. God gives us a choice. If you don't want to amend, then all your evil, even the emotional component, will come back to you in the form of adverse life events. If you wish to continue getting beaten down, that is your choice. Free will. That is why I never force this concept upon anyone; I don't threaten. Otherwise, I would be going against the Law of Freedom of Choice. I simply describe my experience in applying Christianity. I want to be a Christian not because of the beautiful title, but because *it is an entrance into Real Life!* Jesus described this entrance as "I am the way and the truth and the life." (John, 14:6). "I am the gate; whoever enters through Me will be saved." (John, 10:9). Where do we begin the work to achieve this?

When I began exploring religion, I knew that I had to *fully examine and comprehend* this field in order for me to have any accomplishments in spirit. I visited various churches, denominations, cults, esoteric groups, and other spiritual practices, and all I heard were countless beautiful words and empty phrases. Yes, it seemed like many of them had unlocked a hidden power and ability to manage certain high-speed waves. However, soon I began to feel that those waves were used mostly for evil purposes – against competitors or to suppress one's will, which you cannot do. That understanding came to me later; but first, I realized that I am just like everyone else, and my mistakes are registered Up Above and recorded similar to a blueprint: wrong here, wrong here, wrong here. I also did some good things, so my life resembled black and white stripes: good/bad/good/bad, according to the Law of Retribution.

I thought to myself: if the Law of Retribution (cause-and-effect) works, then it's only logical that my problems today are the effect of some cause in my past. I knew I wasn't a saint; thus, I had past violations that must be penalized in order for the Law to work. I took that into consideration, which in science is called "a priori", meaning "before the experience". In religion, they call it "faith". I had no experience yet, so I accepted the Law by default. I conditionally admitted - yes, the Law works. So, if the Law works (what you sow, so must you reap) and today I received a penalty (I was insulted, robbed, deceived, etc.), wouldn't it be the consequence of some past events? If I accept it "de facto", then I have no right to be angry, offended, or depressed. Because what I sowed in the past, I am reaping today. Once upon a time, I was wrong and made someone suffer; thus, today I must suffer in return by the Law of the Highest Justice of this world. If I am honest with myself, I must admit it.

This fundamental Law is always in force and has never ceased to operate, so I decided to verify It. *I started forgiving*. This doesn't mean to simply forgive your offender verbally ("I forgive you!") and give them a smile. Perhaps you even feel on the surface that you really forgave them, but upon looking deeper, there is still lingering resentment inside you. It dwells in you and accumulates over time as you keep getting offended by one person, another one, a third one, and so on. This snowball grows bigger with each passing year. I came to realize that if I honestly wanted to forgive, I had to remove this "splinter"; the grudge had to dissolve entirely, disappear without a trace. I am describing this in a nutshell, but in reality, it took me some time to understand this concept and *to make* my soul forgive, to learn how to do it. There is a big difference between *genuine forgiveness* and *forcing yourself to forgive*. You might convince yourself that you must forgive because it is beneficial for your health, and you shouldn't hold a grudge because you are better than that. However, that approach won't bring any results. For me to achieve genuine forgiveness, I had to clarify to my own brain what was occurring, because my brain is constantly resisting. My brain says, "They strike you, so you strike back! Look what they did to you! Take revenge!" We have grown accustomed to this life stance; we exist this way. But I decided to take a different route. *I've accepted that by the Law, one <u>must</u> hurt me because I hurt someone in the past.* If I have done some bad things, then in return, I must receive some adversities in my life. That is the Law of the Highest Justice of this world - *don't do wrong, and you won't live a troubled life*.

Equipped with that logic, I started forgiving. I stopped being irritated with people. I have learned to forgive sincerely with all of my heart and soul. For this is *the only way* to write off sins. **There is not one church, not one priest, not even a saint that has the ability to forgive you of your sins**, as people have been led to believe. **THAT NOTION IS A TERRIBLE LIE!** There is *one way and one way only* to forgive sin. There is only *one* method that exists on the entire planet. Did any righteous people exist before Christ? Of course, they did. How did they turn from criminals into righteous beings? You can find it in the Old Testament and some other literature describing life before the Old Testament. **Sin is forgiven only one way – by recognizing and accepting that the Law has the right to punish you.** Accept it! This is humility, *real humility*.

The moment I took that position in life and started forgiving, my sins began to dissipate. After 4-5 months, all my serious illnesses practically vanished. I was 46 years old then. Now I am much older, and I have forgotten about doctors, which has made me very happy. That alone is a huge accomplishment! I don't need doctors because the cells of my body transformed into a state of harmony within a few years. All because I accepted everything with humility and continue to do so. I never get mad at people; I don't even get annoyed. I am not afraid of anything. I have neither jealousy nor vanity. When you rid yourself of these vices, inner harmony comes, which is the Light!

4. THE EMBODIED WORD

Despite all the acquired positive changes as a result of eliminating your negative character traits, life can still be very hard at times. This is because the world is not so simple. Maybe you have turned over a new leaf and a few others are following your example, but the rest of the world continues to act the way they want in accordance with the Law of Freedom of Choice. They don't want to change; thus, you receive some taunts and attacks from people. But you can resist it; you have the strength. Jesus once said that if you follow the Commandments, He and the Father will come and make their home with you. *That means protecting you from the rest of the world.* "Anyone who loves Me will obey My teaching. My Father will love them, and we will come to them and make our home with them." (John 14:23). I have experienced that. Slowly, all of those familiar biblical phrases started coming to life within me. I began to understand what Jesus once said to us, which includes myself personally as well as each one of you. *He came to the people of Earth and told them what they needed to do.* Connection with God doesn't come to you by carrying yourselves proudly or praying in public, for God doesn't need this! That isn't how the Connection with God occurs. Jesus said that nobody comes to God other than through Him. "I am the way and the truth and the life. No one comes to the Father except through Me." (John, 14:6). And what was Jesus? *He was the embodied Word!* The Gospel of John states that in the beginning, there was the Word, and the Word was with God, and the Word was God! The Word created the world. The Word created man. Meaning the Word is Light, It is Love, and It supports us, empowering us on this road.

Jesus said He was the embodied Word: "I am the bread of life. Here is the bread that comes down from heaven, which anyone may eat and not die. I am the living bread that came down from heaven. Whoever eats this bread will live forever. This bread is my flesh, which I will give for the life of the world." (John, 6:48-51). "Whoever eats My flesh and drinks My blood has eternal life, and I will raise them up at the last day. For My flesh is real food and My blood is real drink. Whoever eats My flesh and drinks My blood remains in Me, and I in them. Just as the living Father sent Me and I live because of the Father, so the one who feeds on Me will live because of Me. This is the bread that came down from heaven. Your ancestors ate manna and died, but whoever feeds on this bread will live forever." (John, 6:53-58).

1.
I AM THE LORD THY GOD!
THOU SHALT HAVE NO OTHER GODS BUT ME!

2.
THOU SHALT NOT TAKE THE NAME OF THE LORD
THY GOD IN VAIN!

3.
THOU SHALT KEEP THE SABBATH DAY HOLY!

4.
THOU SHALT HONOR FATHER AND MOTHER!

5.
THOU SHALT NOT KILL!

6.
THOU SHALT NOT COMMIT ADULTERY!

7.
THOU SHALT NOT STEAL!

8.
THOU SHALT NOT BEAR FALSE WITNESS
AGAINST THY NEIGHBOR!

9.
DO NOT LET THYSELF LUST AFTER THY
NEIGHBOR'S WIFE!

10.
THOU SHALT NOT COVET THY NEIGHBOR'S
HOUSE, NOR HIS FARM, NOR HIS CATTLE, NOR
ANYTHING THAT IS HIS!

Ill.4

By instructing the disciples to eat the bread, Jesus meant to "eat" His *Word*; take in His Word and live by It! Likewise, when He spoke of drinking His blood, He meant to "drink" His *Word*, making It your way of life! ***This is the true meaning of the Communion!***

God was *embodied* in the human body. But He wasn't the flesh, made up of electrons and protons. He was that Luminescence and Force which people couldn't see but could sense. He had such power of conviction that when He spoke, people believed Him undoubtedly. He either had absolute enemies in those who knew the extent of their wickedness, or absolute admirers. People were immediately divided into either friends or enemies of God. No one was indifferent.

Jesus was the embodiment of Love. God did not give Him orders to punish the Earth, even though He had that power at His disposal. The coming of Christ was the last "therapeutic" attempt to help people. It was the revival of the power of the Word, Its accuracy and truthfulness. He said, "Do not think that I have come to abolish the Law or the Prophets; I have not come to abolish them but to fulfill them." (Matthew, 5:17). He wasn't against Moses; on the contrary, He confirmed his words. However, the Laws of Moses have been so disfigured through more than a thousand years, that again the help of the Higher Force was needed to come and say, "Has not Moses given you the Law? Yet not one of you keeps the Law." (John, 7:19).

Let's talk briefly about the Laws of Moses. Everyone who considers himself a faithful Christian likely knows the Ten Commandments given by Moses (Illustration 4). These Commandments are spiritual guidelines, without which freedom of the soul is unachievable. However, people interpret these crucial guidelines superficially, reducing their significance to the realm of deeds, while completely neglecting the world of thoughts and feelings. For instance, take the fifth Commandment, "Thou shalt not kill!" This Commandment is simply interpreted as do not commit a murder of physical flesh. But read the Commandment again! Does it state that specifically? No. *Killing* is a broad, comprehensive concept. Certainly, physical murder is considered killing, but it is not limited to just that. Here is an example of what I mean. A young man is dreaming about becoming a doctor. His father, however, has other hopes for him. The boy comes from a family of attorneys, and the father wants him to continue the tradition.

GOD
THE TRUTH

Jesus Christ

John the Baptist
Moses, Zoroaster
Krishna

Primordial
Spiritual World

Secondary
Spiritual World

THE LINE OF PROPHETS

wall of negative
emotions and
pseudo-teachings

wall of materialism

layer of sins

The son is then put under great pressure to submit to his father's will, abandoning his personal calling to become a doctor. Consequently, he invests years of hard work in studying and practicing the profession he has no passion for, perhaps not even benefiting society in any way, on top of ruining his own life. He was granted a gift from God through the natural talent of healing people and saving lives, which dwelled inside, urging him to pursue a career as a physician. But that gift was buried under his father's pressure. Do you see what happened here? To kill means *to deaden*. Here we see that the father committed a severe offence against the Commandment "Thou shalt not kill!" One may not only kill the body, but also a dream, a great talent, a genuine passion, and so on. You may read more in depth about each of the Ten Commandments in the book *The Ten Commandments of God and the Lord's Prayer* by Abd-Ru-Shin.

When Jesus came, He started speaking in the language of the soul. His Line of Light started creating vibrations in people's souls, which were detached from the Light on the level of the Astral World (Illustration 5). What is a Prophet, or any Messenger from Above, as a phenomenon? The Prophet is the one who breaks through the murky astral filth and all the "dark clouds" of our sins. He comes and his Line of Light is protected by the Holy Spirit so that he can deliver the Truth. Not one creature on Earth can get to the Truth on their own because people are unable to hold such a corridor of protection. And only the Holy Spirit can support a man in his procession upward.

We are engulfed with garbage by our sins, and it is impossible to break through this crust without help from Above. That is why Prophets have become more common in the last millennia. Finally, it has been said: if you cannot cope with the help provided, then your end will come! Just like in the old Russian saying: "Only the grave will remedy the hunchback!" You bring evil into this world and you are not willing to change. Look at this world! The ecology is ruined. You poisoned both water and air. Not only are you destroying yourselves but also the animal kingdom and the natural world. What do you expect?! You cannot go on like this! What are your motives? What are your end goals? You strive for money and comfort above all else. You want a good life, but you won't attain it. Look at Illustration 3, "The Law of Retribution", again. If you project it onto the billions of Earth's population, no one is willing to accept their misfortunes with humility, **which means there is no redemption of sins**. Thus, we are accumulating more and more; eventually, the critical mass will reach its limit and then collapse. That is what is referred to as the Last Judgment. How much longer can this human-generated mayhem be tolerated? After all, the vast majority are not willing to change. This is the reason for the Judgment and Its necessity.

In my spiritual work, I wanted to become a person who would no longer be punished by the Law. For this is the function of the Law: to punish criminals until they reform and to protect people who obey It from those who do not. And that is exactly what I have experienced! But it doesn't mean I am ignoring the rest of the world. On the contrary, I realized that if I have learned to do this, I can now pass this experience on to others, which I gradually started doing. Naturally, this experience accrues year after year. The longer you live this way, the more you come to understand that this is *the only cure, the only way out* of the swamp we have fallen into and continue sinking. That is the way for many people and not just for one individual. However, it cannot be imposed on anyone. Otherwise, one would be going against the Law of Freedom of Choice - one of the fundamental Laws of the Creation.

5. UNDERSTANDING WHAT IS EVIL IN YOU

Besides the Law of Freedom of Choice and the Law of Retribution or "what you sow, that you shall reap", which Indians call the Law of Karma, there are other Laws: the Law of Motion, the Law of Resemblance, the Law of Attraction, the Law of Separation.

The Law of Motion requires us to move if we want to stay physically and spiritually healthy. We must be agile with our bodies through exercise, with our brain through continuously expanding our knowledge, and with our spirit through spiritual development. Stagnation on any level will eventually lead to a disintegration of our being.

The Law of Resemblance comes into play through the process of incarnation of the human soul, which will be covered in more detail later in this book. Additionally, the Law of Resemblance has another function. It allows you to draw in demons similar to your own. The word "demons" is a simple term to describe the ugly and harmful forms *created by emitting any negative emotions*. When you generate negative emotions, not only do you create those forms, but you also make "holes" in your protective armor. Then, by the Law of Resemblance, similar demons are pulled into your field, causing misfortune and bad health. You began this journey and already made a few steps towards amending yourself, but you are still "raw", and those demons can still reach you. First, they are coming from your past as unredeemed sins. Second, your immediate mistakes also condemn you to some suffering. The main thing is not to get discouraged and to ask for protection through the Lord's Prayer when the going gets tough.

The Law of Attraction can be observed when people gravitate towards each other based on their interests: drunks associate with other drunks, bikers socialize with each other, nature lovers form hiking groups, and so on.

The Law of Separation makes itself evident when you see an apple falling from a tree, or when a mother gives birth to a child, or when a butterfly leaves its cocoon. Likewise, a man sheds his cloaks when he first leaves the Physical World, then the Ethereal World, then the Sphere of Animistic Substantiality, making his way up to his *real home* – the World of Pure Spirits, which people refer to as Paradise. So, he is separating from his physical body, then the ethereal body, then the animistic cloak as he ascends to his origin. Then all he has left is his pure spirit. But the final destination isn't granted freely, *it must be earned*.

You can find more information about the Laws in the book *In the Light of Truth* by Abd-Ru-Shin. When I learned these Laws through my own experience, I started building my life based *upon Them* as opposed to my education. Our education, if one learned anything and applied it to their life, only pertains to earth, to our intellectual skills in order to meet our basic needs and to earn and manage our assets. However, there are other concepts in life, such as good fortune, physical health, and favorable circumstances, in opposition to constantly stumbling on one obstacle after another. Those concepts lie in the field of spirituality and depend solely on whether or not we obey the Laws of God. *If you want to be happy, stop breaking the Laws!* You have already accumulated hundreds of thousands of sins by breaking the Laws in the past, and each one requires redemption.

Esoteric groups and many Christian denominations say, "God is punishing us. We are not righteous, we are sinful; thus, we have a hard life and we must endure it." Yes, of course, we must endure it and accept with humility the results of our wrongdoings. *But we must also stop the wrongdoings!* We can erase our old sins through humility. But if we do so while continuing to commit new sins at the same time, then we keep adding to the old foundation of transgressions. What is the point in sweeping leaves under the trees in autumn? They will only continue to fall. So, our lives are constantly in shambles. Then it becomes a perpetual battle with yourself. Wouldn't it be much wiser to stop creating evil? But first, you need to understand what exactly inside of you is evil.

We think that if we are rude to someone, or if we strike someone, or steal from someone – that is bad, that is a sin. And if we feel offended or annoyed, angry or scared, we think it is not a sin. *But that is also a sin.* We all live this way, and we cannot understand why our health suffers, why we have bad joints, aching backs, bad blood vessels, and all manner of ailments. I don't consider myself a bad person, but I once counted an average of 30 mistakes I made in a day. And not with my words or deeds, but with my *inner world*. *My thoughts and feeling were wrong.* I multiplied 30 by 365 days in a year and multiplied that number by 31, the conscious years of my life. I was 46 years old at the time; I subtracted 15 unconscious years, because a child may not be held accountable at such a young age. So, I calculated about 350,000 sins. *Those are the evil forms that I released into this world.* They were all mine, *and each and every one of them required redemption.* They all laid heavy on my soul, manifesting as health ailments. When I started living by the Laws, absolutely everything health-wise came to a norm, including my spine. I used to be an athlete playing the notoriously rough sport of rugby, which resulted in a very bad back due to multiple injuries. I had many health problems, and now they are all gone. In a matter of a few months, my spine became like new again. This might seem miraculous to anyone who is ignorant in this field. However, there is nothing out of the ordinary about it. *I simply stopped battling with the Law of God - the unsurpassable Force that will crush anyone who tries to resist It.* Thus, I verified through my experience that if I accept my fate with humility, I *myself* can eliminate my accrued Karma, only because I now took the right stand in life. That is obeying the Law of Retribution. I told you for a reason that when you get upset with someone, you are not willing to accept the punishment handed through that person. If we were wrong in the past, then who will deliver us the resulting punishment today? Some person will present a situation from which we will suffer because we *also* created such situations in the past. And now by the Law of the Highest Justice, which is controlled by the Creator, the punishment is *inevitable*.

Naturally, the sacramental question arises: "Why doesn't God start punishing bad people first?" Why do some live luxuriously despite the fact that they have robbed and devastated whole nations? They have sucked funds like leaches, and we all know it. So, why do they go unpunished? I will explain.

6. UMBRELLA OF PROTECTION

Let's turn to Illustration 6. There is God, the Creator, that radiates. This radiation is the Law, the Lines of Force. All people under these Lines of Force are not distorting them by their wrong personal motives - they live strictly by the Law. Such a person stands under the "umbrella of protection". The Law *protects* him. He is a *righteous* man, by the fact that he is living *right*. People who stand near to the umbrella are your average good people, representing most of the population. Farther away from the umbrella are people worse than the ordinary, and even farther away are the crooks, cruel people, murderers, organizers of persecutions and many other adverse events on a global scale. They have walked very far from the Law. So, what happens in the area that is not under the umbrella? *The Law controls it but doesn't help people, because they are breaking the Law!* The ordinary people are breaking the Law a little and the horrible people - considerably more. Figuratively speaking, you are stealing twenty dollars from God, and the worst ones are stealing twenty million. They are breaking the Law immeasurably more than you are, but *both* are considered criminals. Just like in prison. All criminals are different: some are sentenced to one year in prison, some to life, but they are all criminals. And the Law cannot protect criminals. Whether you are a minor criminal or a major one, you are still a criminal.

Moreover, you are a repeat offender. You have lived this way your entire life, and you are unwilling to change. What do you expect out of life then? In this world, *you are not the one in charge* but the Will of God that is in control. And It will *always* punish the one who has taken even as little as two or three wrong stands. Following, the *nearly* righteous people wonder why their life is so hard.

Here the Law of Motion comes into play: move towards God, and the beating will slowly stop. And that is what I have done. I thought it would take at least 10-30 years of hard work for me to see any progress - that was the experience of our saints. It turned out that it was enough just to *start moving*. I told myself, "I believe in God! There is God, there is I, and there is the way to the Light!" and I started moving. I made my soul a priority. I began to change; thereby, God started turning towards me. I moved from my standstill, thus obeying the Law of Motion. What was the purpose of us coming to Earth? We came to evolve. So, I started developing, evolving in spirit; in addition, I chose God by the Law of Freedom of Choice.

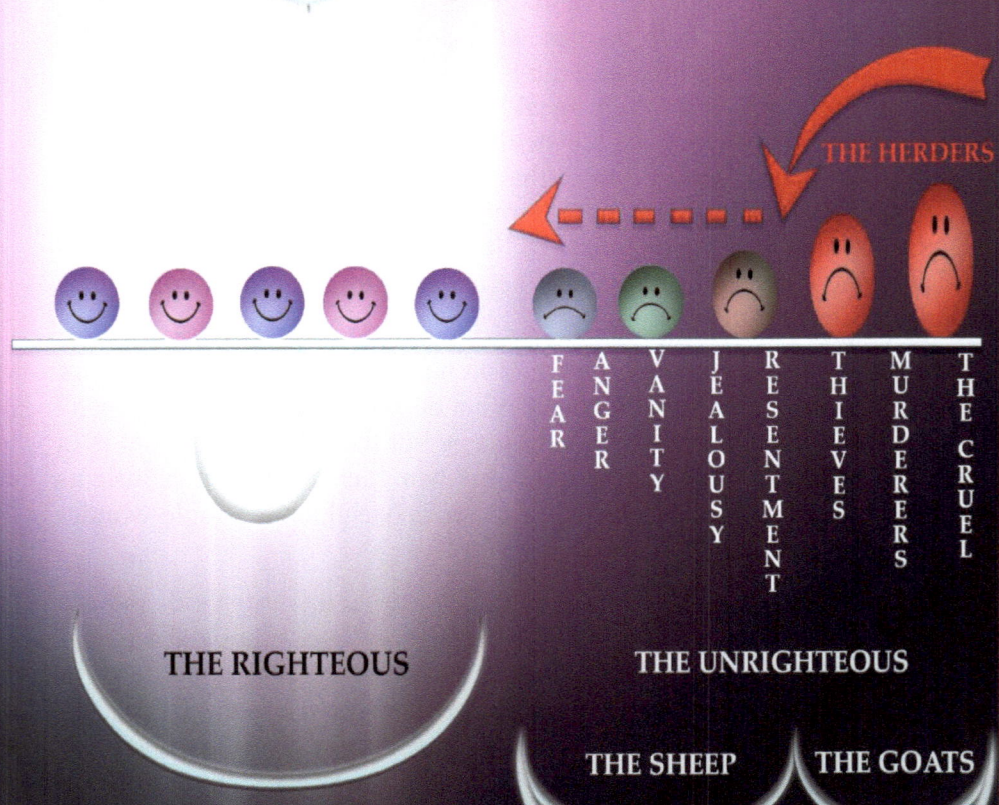

GOD

THE LAW

THE HERDERS

F E A R
A N G E R
V A N I T Y
J E A L O U S Y
R E S E N T M E N T
T H I E V E S
M U R D E R E R S
T H E C R U E L

THE RIGHTEOUS

THE UNRIGHTEOUS

THE SHEEP

THE GOATS

OUTSIDE THE LAW

III.6

I did not choose to maintain that I am an exceptional being, that my life is unique, and that I am the master of this life, so I can do what I please; I can do bad things and no one will see it. Instead, the Law always sees and will punish me. In this way, there is nothing that goes unredeemed. Retribution always catches up with you. So, why doesn't God start His punishment with bad people?

The average people are relatively good. The fewer mistakes people make, the better they are, which means the closer they stand to the umbrella of protection. Naturally, there are very few of these people. I was roughly an average person before; I wasn't cruel, greedy, or envious. I did not scheme on any level, either through work or the government. However, the pack of people who walked too far from the Law ("the herders", Illustration 6) was crushing me, creating an unbearable life. I was materialistic until the age of 46. That was when I decided to investigate and started moving in the direction of the Law. The squad of the herders *forced me* to do this. And I know now why Jesus said, "But I tell you, love your enemies" (Matthew, 5:44). I bless mine from the bottom of my heart because if it weren't for them, I would never have started moving in the direction of faith. Who pushed me to do that? My enemies did! And I understood why God doesn't start with them: ***bad people are like a stick that herds us under the Law***. I realized that they have an essential role in this world. They poison our lives, but we should not be angry with them, as strange as it sounds. They are also doing useful work. They can only reach and agitate the lazy ones, those who march on the streets with slogans: "Give us retirement! Give us benefits! Let's make our country great! Give us this and give us that…" Nobody will give them anything because, by God's Law, none of them can be assured of justice or a decent life in this world as they are sinners and *continue* to sin, at least with their emotions. So, they will always be beaten, and beaten, and beaten as they get even angrier when a blow of fate strikes them. These jabs come from the herders as well. *And instead of turning to forgiveness and moving towards God, they do just the opposite.* Millions, tens and hundreds of millions of people throughout the world live this way. Thus, they are not moving towards God – so the battering continues.

I was forced to start my spiritual investigation back in 1994; life required it. I felt I was at the end of my rope: my health was falling apart, my career came to an end, my country was in shambles, and there were crises everywhere I looked. So, there I stood amid this nightmare, pitiful, sick, and nearing my last breath. What was there to do, where could I turn to? Anywhere I went, I either had to bribe someone or furnish money I didn't have. There was only racketeering and corruption and nowhere to go. At last, I cried out, "God, help me!" Then, as if God said to me, "Finally, you need Me. You thought you were doing just fine without Me all those years, and now, when your life is in ruins, you need Me. Very well, I will help you on one condition - learn to live by the Law. The Law will help you if you *really* respect and obey It." I am describing this sort of fictional dialogue in my own words, of course, but in its essence, that is precisely what happened.

Understand that we have a traditional approach to life out of habit. We think we are the victims of many circumstances. We are the victims of dishonest people who have organized our society in terrible ways; we have a bad family life, and things, in general, are going wrong. We think there are enemies and rivals everywhere. The truth is, there is only *one* enemy - **man is his own enemy.** We carry on a perpetual fight with ourselves, and our misfortunes and bad health are proof of that.

7. KEEP THE HEARTH
OF YOUR THOUGHTS PURE!

When a righteous person standing under the umbrella of God's protection breaks the Law, he slowly starts losing that protection. If the person is afraid, he takes one step out from under the umbrella. If he is jealous or irritable, vain or envious, he takes many steps away from this protection. This is how he gradually travels far away from the umbrella. But he walks away *voluntarily. After millions of years, man has gone so far that he no longer knows his way back!* Thus, to return, he needs to have very clear and precise directions. A long time ago, those directions were given by the Prophets. They came to help us multiple times. Those were Krishna, Zoroaster, and Moses (Illustration 5). They all were messengers from God. Finally, Jesus Christ came. And they all said the same thing: *obey the Commandments!* The Commandments must be obeyed not only in deeds and words, but also in keeping our thoughts and feelings pure. *Keep the hearth of your thoughts pure!* Meaning, we must also pay attention to the inner world. It is as if God says, "You, the materialists, think you are accountable only for your actions and words. You look good on the surface, but you are rotten on the inside! You think wickedly. You emit negative emotions, even though on the exterior you look calm and collected. This is what's called 'the hypocrisy'! You may act friendly and kind, but on the inside, you are burning with anger and other negative emotions. And that is a sin. When I control this world, not only do I control the world of your acts and words but also of your thoughts and feelings. These are My creations. I created all of these domains, and they are *Mine!* So, a violation on *any* level is a sin and not only on the levels of words and deeds. Your point of view is wrong. My point of view as the Creator and Supervisor of this world is different. Your thoughts and feelings are also under close scrutiny. And if you aren't victorious on these two levels, you will perish." You all consider yourselves righteous, and everyone is bad except *you*. But it is not clear why your life isn't so great. The reason is that, unfortunately, you don't understand how to fight your demons on the level of your thoughts and feelings.

When the Prophets came, they all taught exactly this. But the armies of those who called themselves priests mutilated this knowledge. They included the seemingly correct motives, such as "you have to live by the Commandments", but in reality, they distorted the teaching. With each subsequent arrival of the Prophets, the priests would take their teachings and morph them into imprecise instructions, leaving some part from God and some part from themselves. Therefore, the Truth was diluted and transformed into something indigestible. All they preach are beautiful words. Jesus referred to this as *"giving rocks instead of bread"*. What did He call those priests 2000 years ago? "You are like whitewashed tombs, which look beautiful on the outside, but on the inside are full of the bones of the dead and everything unclean." (Matthew, 23:27). "The teachers of the Law and the Pharisees sit in Moses' seat. So, you must be careful to do everything they tell you. But do not do what they do, for they do not practice what they preach." (Matthew, 23:2,3). Jesus *demanded* that the people live according to the Law. When He revealed that He was not of this world by showing great miracles, people realized that God was before them. Then He instructed not to listen to those priests but to listen to Him.

One must enter religion not through their exterior splendor but through their inner world. In other words, we must rebuild our psyche. I am putting in modern terms what Christ once said. *We must know how to keep our thoughts and feelings pure*. Once again, in order to explain to our foolish mind where we are wrong, we must seriously examine this topic. I first had to explain to my brain why my resentment, irritability, and anger are considered a sin. It is because my reaction to the blow of fate is wrong. With this strike, a sin is written off *only* when I internally say, "God, thank You!" Rather than being upset, I say, "A sin is written off through this experience." The opposite reaction would be resentment, anger, or vindictiveness, demanding immediate restoration of justice: let my offender suffer too, since I am suffering! I may not be thinking about it, but the emotion is there. This is the silent *demand* you're presenting to God: "God, You have missed that they are beating on me, your beloved son. Hit them on the head and preferably harder, *the way I want!*" Thus, we put ourselves *above* God and start demanding with our emotions without realizing it. This moment needs to be explained to people, for it is extremely important. It means that we are constantly in the state of "God-fighting". In reality, we are against God, although many consider themselves religious believers, regular churchgoers, and God worshipers. But the fact is, this emotion of dissatisfaction is an *unconscious opposition to God*. It is simply out of ignorance, which arises on the basis of spiritual laziness, meaning our unwillingness to examine these issues. I wanted to stop this opposition because I realized that unless I accomplish this, not only will I never emerge out of the sea of misfortunes, but I will eventually perish in it forever.

I repeat, I want to be a Christian not because of the beautiful title, but because it is a gateway into a true Life! To enter through it, one must first have faith. Why did Jesus say, "Truly I tell you, unless you change and become like little children, you will never enter the Kingdom of Heaven." (Matthew, 18:3)? Because a child isn't yet "marred" by intellect. When a child believes in something, he does so without reservation. His faith is genuine because his intellect isn't working in opposition to it. He believes wholeheartedly. The difference between a child and me is that I am an educated person. I have two technical diplomas plus a medical one. In sum, these credentials do not provide release from a bad life. Thus, it's not about education. All my life, I considered myself a man with strong will. I've accomplished many things. I held a leading position at work. I worked abroad for many years. I have achieved everything on my own. I had enough will, patience, aspiration, and perseverance. I loved studying because I knew why I needed it. All of that did not provide me with a good life. Upon realizing this, I concluded that something was off. I started searching in a different place, and I found it.

At first, I didn't even realize that I was exploring religion. I thought I was conducting some esoteric experiments. I had investigated esotericism for a while and felt that what they were offering wasn't the pure teaching. With all the ranting about honesty, decency, the lack of vanity and greed, they do not live by those assertions. That is called hypocrisy. It's when a person says one thing, but on the inside, he does another. If you want to be honest, you must do what you say. And when you do as you speak, then your word is filled with the power of Light. But if you don't act according to what you preach, then the Light refuses you in support. Your word becomes *weak*.

How do the priests throughout history work? They speak on Earth, quoting the Prophets. They are quoting word for word. However, they themselves are not trying to obey the Commandments. Or, they might be trying, but not succeeding at it. Thus, they only reach the realm of thoughts or, at most, the Astral World. They are receiving information from those realms only. *But the human soul is higher than that.* And the souls of those priests are locked from them because they are cut off by the undefeated vices, *which is the failure to obey the Commandments.* The same occurs with a person who comes to their churches. He is also blocked by his sins.

That person would like to change and is seeking answers from the church. He arrives and says, "Teach me to live by the Commandments." They respond with, "You must read about the experience of the elders." If he comes to esotericism, they offer to read such books as *Anastasia*, or *Bhagavat Gita*, or *Kundalini Yoga*, and so on. Everyone offers different things, depending on the trend. *But those gurus have not fought their own demons. All those teachers have sins.* Some have more than others. What happens in this case? How can a teacher get through to a soul that is blocked by sins? Who is capable of galvanizing the human soul to battle its own sins? Only the one who *himself* has had a breakthrough! The one who has broken through the crust of his sins and connected his soul with his body; that is, of course, with the help of God's Will! (Illustration 7, the walls of negative emotions and pseudo-teachings). *Then* his words spoken on Earth are filled with the power of the Light of the soul. And behind that soul stands God, saying, "You are telling the truth! You do what you preach." Then he *delivers* this *strong* Word here on Earth. And only such a Word has the power of reaching other souls.

But if you don't do what you say, you will be *"giving rocks instead of bread"*, as Jesus said, because you yourself did not break through to your own soul. This expression is just as valid today as it was 2000 years ago. Many can speak eloquently, from politicians to the clergy. *But those words are dead.* They do not deliver anything. They do not uplift. When a person who has broken through the blockage of his sins speaks, his soul vibrates because it is connected with the Light. His soul is fighting! And when you are linked with your soul, you start broadcasting on *all* levels! Remember that your spirit has cloaks (Illustration 2). So, your cloaks begin translating onto the cloaks of a person you are reaching. Then your listener responds with their soul. *That* is the uplift! If this is not done, and you speak only on the lower levels without breaking through to your soul, you won't raise anyone to battle. This is the defeat of all the churches! They justified the impossibility of entering into the Spiritual World by quoting Paul or others. ***But Jesus said, "If you love Me, keep My Commands."*** This is the installation from God! It's the installation of the <u>founder</u> of the Christian Church - Jesus Christ, the One who said, *"If you love Me, keep My Commands"*! What comes next? *Keep the hearth of your thoughts pure.* Meaning, you must be pure *on all levels of your being*. Not only your thoughts but also your emotions must be pure. Then you are connecting, you are in touch with God. ***This connection is religion!***

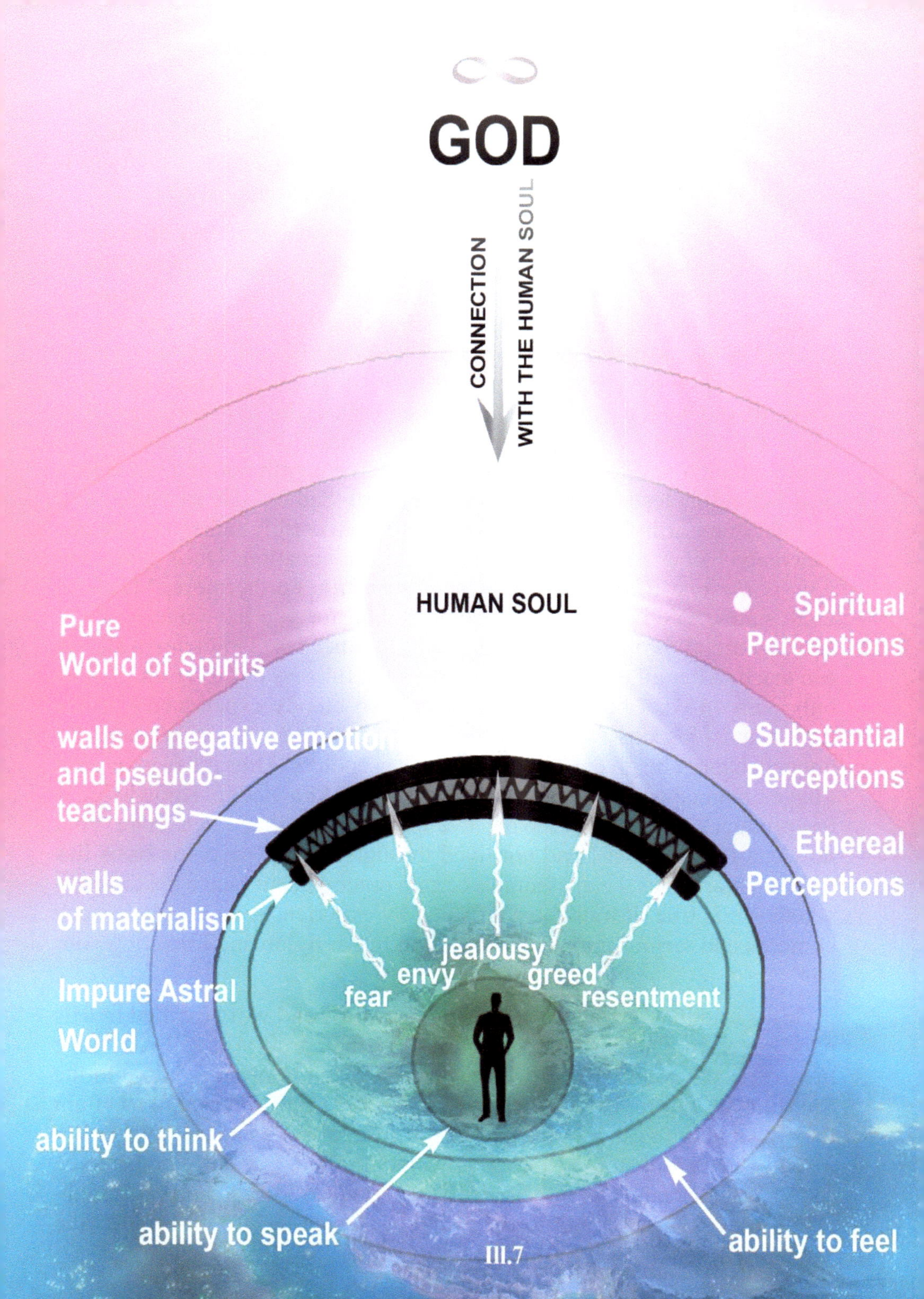

GOD

CONNECTION WITH THE HUMAN SOUL

HUMAN SOUL

● **Spiritual Perceptions**

Pure World of Spirits

● **Substantial Perceptions**

walls of negative emotion and pseudo-teachings

● **Ethereal Perceptions**

walls of materialism

jealousy

envy   greed

fear   resentment

Impure Astral World

ability to think

ability to speak

ability to feel

III.7

Because the word "religion" translates to "restoring the connection". The prefix "re" means "recovery", like RE-novation, RE-incarnation, and RE-storation. That is the restoration of something. In this case, RE-ligion is restoration of the Higher Connection. This Connection must be *real*.

Observe how extensively evil and lies permeate the subject of religion. There exists literature that describes how the Church made up many things. It is shocking to read the extent of how false this system is! For instance, it describes how the priests assigned themselves the right to be priests. Jesus said in the Gospel of Matthew, 23:9, "And do not call anyone on earth 'father' for you have one Father, and He is in Heaven." That's how it is written! And we have "holy fathers" in churches. *But holy is the one who obeys the Commandments.* Then the "holy father" is a usurpation of the term without a real foundation. It is just a screen, with nothing but emptiness behind it. Jesus forbade saying the word "father". He said you have no father on Earth; He is Up Above. There is an earthly father and the one Heavenly Father. A priest is irrelevant in the equation. Once again, *the holy is the one who obeys the Commandments.* Furthermore, Matthew, 23:8, states, "You are not to be called Rabbi, for you have one Teacher, and you are all brothers." Jesus spoke it. It is because God knows all. He can teach. After all, a man cannot possess the fullness of the Truth. He can only pass on what he has gained in his own bloody experience – in the fight against his sins. What he gained, only that he can give. What he did not gain cannot be given. That experience is endless. Thus, I can give what I have obtained and understood clearly through knowledge. Knowledge is the product of experience. What I've experienced, that I can share. And how can I share what I had not lived through? In that case, the basis lies only in theory. Yes, I can assume a certain outcome, but I have yet to verify whether it is true. It must be confirmed by experience, especially in such complex and serious matters as understanding religion and liberating your soul.

Jesus said that they will speak with His words and will be called by His name, even by the Christian churches. "By their fruit you will recognize them." (Matthew, 23:16). Christian churches *do not* bring a man into the Spiritual World; they do not give that *entrance* Jesus referred to as "I am the way and the truth and the life"! And what about esoteric groups? For instance, let's look at the Roerich movement. There is a lot of praise to be found in their texts. Open the book *Agni Yoga*, and you'll find stunningly beautiful texts. Something to the effect of, "Friends, let's do it, let's take the upper ways to the Light! We are bhaktas…" They have their own terminology. "Come on, let's go, let's go, come on…!" That is where it ends. But where is *the how*? It turns out, *this is a void* decorated in a very nice package. To top it all, when you dig deeper into the Roerichs, the biographies of Helena, Nicholas, or the followers (their sons), you will find family strife and the ugly divisions of property after the death of Nicholas Roerich. What kind of Prophets are those?! Or take Blavatsky, who was a pure devil's advocate. There was a documentary about her, describing how she lived in America for a while, and how she got married at a very young age for the sole purpose of acquiring the status of a married woman. Shortly after, she left her husband and used his assets, which she attained after the divorce. Using her status as a married woman, she traveled abroad to start her "Mahatmas", and off it went. She trampled on her husband's fate and from the wreckage, she launched her career as a pseudo-prophet. This is Theosophy. Then you read her work on how God is "bad", and Satan is "good". She writes that Satan opened our eyes and gave us the occult knowledge. He is Prometheus. He gave this knowledge, bypassing gods. Right! Bypassing God, he gave a man knowledge, which led to occultism and to the professional casting of spells, speaking in simple terms. That is what Satan did. And she called him Prometheus, whereas God made the defective goods - bad Adam and bad Eve. Why does a man commit evil? She suggests that God created Adam, who was defective. God created a bad man who is unable to do good. What she doesn't understand is that man was given freedom of choice. However, man is using this freedom very poorly.

A man was granted free will, according to the Law of Freedom of Choice. And what if a man was denied freedom of choice? Let's assume that man was bound only to do good. Refer to Illustration 2, showing man as a seed in the Spiritual World and presume that he can *only* do good. However, don't forget that man was a weak creature. He wasn't even a "man" yet, but a seed. He must become spiritually strong and conscious, eventually transforming himself into a complete human being. How would one gain consciousness without having the freedom of choice? If everything he ever does is good, he will fall asleep and think "I'm asleep, and that's already good. I do nothing, and that's good. I spit in the well – good. I kick a dog – good. I cut someone's head off – also good. I don't even have to think or put any effort into being good." But we must develop, and development is always a struggle. It's a strain of your brain and your heart. And straining is putting forth an effort to figure things out, to learn. Thus, if we don't have a choice to do bad, what happens to our freedom of choice and to our right to err?

Man was given free reign over choice. Here are the Creation and the Laws for you. If you do bad, your life will lead you to trouble. If you do good, life will lead you to prosperity. A person must choose. Do good, and that good will give you a great life a hundredfold. Then what are you pleading for from God? Why are you constantly crying "God help me!"? How can He help you if you are continuously harming this world and not even realizing it? Stop the harm! Then your life will blossom with health and happiness! But you don't want to do it! You aren't willing to even try to understand the Laws of your Creator! You have no time for it! You are too busy making money, raising children, and striving for comfort. Thus, you have closed yourselves off from God through your personal problems. You turned religion into a hobby. "Did I go to church? Yes, I did! Did I light a candle? Yes! Did I observe a fast? Yes! I pray as much as my priest told me to." And that's that. What kind of religion is this? This is formalism! It has nothing to do with religion! It's the formality of assigning a man to some denomination. A denomination is a personal view of a group of people on the relationship between man and God. But the truth is, *there is one religion for all on Earth; one God and one religion - obey the Commandments!*

8. SEEKING THE KINGDOM OF HEAVEN

When I stopped my wrongdoings and redeemed my old sins with humility, I noticed that within 4-5 months, nearly all of my serious illnesses left my body. I received something like a brand-new body. After another 10-12 months, my life became much more favorable, and I started experiencing incredible fortune. I began to live a good life. I started making excellent money without straining, and everything was unfolding before me. It was as if some "mechanism" was turned on. Then, I finally understood what Jesus had told His disciples. All of His phrases became a new discovery to me. "So do not worry, saying 'What shall we eat?' or 'What shall we drink?' or 'What shall we wear?' For the pagans run after all these things, and your heavenly Father knows that you need them. But seek first His Kingdom and His righteousness, and all these things will be given to you as well." (Matthew, 6:31-33). I began looking for the Kingdom of Heaven through the way I just told you, in my own words. I started to diminish my wrongdoings and redeemed the biggest mistakes I had committed in the past. It is *impossible* to become righteous overnight. It is impossible to turn into an ideal person so quickly. It is a *long* process. But when you start walking the walk, fighting your demons, and conquering what is dealt to you each day, you can emerge as a winner in any situation. Or you can lose again. Know that you cannot win everywhere at first because your spiritual strength accumulates gradually, step by step. It requires many years of hard work.

When I began experiencing the positive changes in my life, I realized that I had finally gotten it right, and the rest was just a matter of time. The goal was never to permit myself to cool down at any point, veering off this path and allowing laziness to take hold. The Law continuously helps me to stay on this road. The minute I start slowing down, thinking I have accomplished everything, including great health and more desirable life, immediately the problems start to appear. It is as if someone is telling me, "Don't you slow down, keep going! Are you a saint?" To which I respond, "No." "Then keep working! There is still a great gap between what you are today and the ideal, and you must constantly work on reducing that distance. That is the requirement." I asked, "When will this condition be satisfied?" and was told "Never. You will never be able to become an absolute saint, for only God is truly holy. You will perpetually exist in the state of refinement." That is the Law of Motion - one of the fundamental Laws.

As long as a man is moving forward in his evolution and going in the right direction, he will be fine. If he starts slowing down or stops, that is when problems arise.

In the first few years, I used to get very tired, thinking "Will it ever end?! For how much longer I have to keep struggling?!" And I was told, "It will never end." Only later, when I got used to this rhythm, did I realize what a great blessing this is. You are always moving forward, constantly changing, and your life is unfolding differently each time. Your life will never be monotonous or dull. Over time, you become more accurate in understanding this life. Then you begin to marvel at the beauty and the fairness of this world. And sincerely, from the bottom of your heart, you begin to thank the Creator: "Thank you, God, for this beautiful world and Your incredibly wise Laws! I was just a pawn in this process by my own hand." I was ignorant, and my ignorance was the byproduct of my indolence. I was lazy! They call laziness "the mother of all vices" for a reason. Once I shook off my spiritual laziness (not physical, not intellectual, but spiritual), I started exploring the subject of religion and received in abundance. Only practice and experience can lead to these changes. We can talk about religion all day, quoting the Bible or some other great books and people, but it won't bring any results if we don't put it to practice.

9. DIVIDE AND CONQUER

Before Christ, there were no Gospels. Many decades passed after Christ before the Gospels appeared. The word "gospel" translates from Greek as "the good news". People called it "the good news" for the right reason. Eventually, there were only four evangelicals left; but previously, tens of thousands of memoirs were written about Christ. The first attempt to summarize the Gospels took place in the 2nd century, but they began to be composed at the beginning of the 4th century. The four evangelicals were Matthew, Mark, Luke, and John. Had they known that their texts would be canonized, legitimized, and presented as an *absolute truth* to people, they probably would have flinched and said, "What are you doing?! We cannot guarantee the exact words of Jesus. We remember *approximately* what He was saying 20-30 years ago." Keep in mind, the first Gospels were written approximately 30-35 years after Christ's death. Can you remember precisely what your professor told you back in college? Sure, some key phrases may have imprinted in your memory, but many details are likely murky. Even Jesus told His disciples, "I have much more to say to you, more than you can now bear." (John, 16:12). *More than you can now bear!* Because a man is unable to absorb it all at once. Had Jesus not been murdered, perhaps His disciples in the stretch of 10-20 years would have become spiritually strong enough to start passing on their knowledge without distortion. But Jesus Christ was killed, and from that, the fable was born as if He practically *voluntarily* ascended on the cross. In reality, the disciples began so quickly misrepresenting the Message of Jesus, that the Line of Light abandoned them a year later. There is a testimony to that.

Creation receives a powerful impulse of charge each year, which takes place around the celebration of Trinity and the holiday of the White Dove. Historically, these two holidays are very close together. People change those dates from time to time, but this impulse comes at the end of May/beginning of June. It is a flash that gives new energy to the Creation. The Light charges the Creation. This charge happens once a year, in one turn around the Sun. The disciples *sensed* this descent of the Holy Spirit fifty days after Christ's death, which brought on the holiday of Pentecost. There is a religious cult named after it. However, this descent happens every year, but the disciples stopped sensing it one year later. They no longer felt this strike of Light. *With that, God refused them in His Connection because they started spreading lies*. Alongside the Truth that Jesus taught them, they started telling their own versions increasingly as time went by. There were some serious deviations, and God cannot support people in their lies.

Thus, predicting the consequences of such distortion of Christ's Word, the next act of God was described in the last chapter of the New Testament called "Revelation". The chapter starts with what Jesus Christ is telling John through an angel about the future on Earth - the famous Apocalypse. That is in the 1st chapter and the 1st verse. In the 2nd chapter, the 2nd verse of "Revelation", there is a terrible phrase regarding the disciples. Jesus tells John and through John to us, "I know your deeds and your hard work and your perseverance. I know that you cannot tolerate wicked people, that you have tested those who claim to be apostles but are not and have found them false." So, Jesus Christ *Himself* calls the disciples liars. They did not withstand the trial of time, and instead of conquering their own faults, they started pompously distributing what they themselves had very vaguely understood. Consequently, the distortion was commingled with the pure teaching of Christ. First, the lies originated from the apostles, which were later laid into the foundation of mistakes replicated by many Christian denominations. *That is the reason there are so many Christian denominations.* You would think that since there was only one teaching, one Jesus, one God, and man by birth is one (we are all of the same origin), then there shouldn't be any divergences among us. Nevertheless, we are divided into denominations, sub-denominations, cults, spiritual groups, and so on. That is Satan's idea - *divide and conquer*.

Leo Tolstoy wrote in one of his pamphlets that in order to confuse men, Satan told his demons to take a bucket containing hundreds of thousands of seeds, wherein only one seed holds the Truth. Now, throw the bucket of seeds towards the people and they won't find the right one, for all seeds look very much alike. The words are often good, but the deeds are bad. That is why Jesus warned us once, "Watch out for false prophets. They come to you in sheep's clothing, but inwardly they are ferocious wolves." (Matthew, 7:11). Meaning, *the words are of sheep, and the deeds are of wolves.* This applies to politics as well as the spiritual field. If politicians can steal from us politically and economically and commit atrocities to our country, then in spirit, there are far more frightening things occurring.

10. CONNECTING MAN WITH HIS SOUL

Unfortunately, a man is rather materialistic and is mainly concerned with his body, finances, land, and how he can lead a more comfortable life. In his quest to build a foundation for his children and grandchildren, he completely forgot about his soul. He forgot that his soul came to Earth as a traveler, and this is its temporary home. It needs to learn to live in the body, understand the Laws of the Creator, and later leave this place.

What is the whole purpose of our coming to Earth? Refer to Illustration 7. It is impossible to draw a complex, multidimensional parallel world. But we need some picture of it, so this graph is just a simplified means of describing it. There is the pure World of Spirits, and there is the impure Astral World. It is impure because any feelings of resentment, fear, envy, greed, and other negative emotions are being pushed out into the Astral World. These emotions are all near us, suspended in the air as created forms. God gave us the ability to create, and we create forms. Unfortunately, we often create evil without knowing it. We ourselves created this impure world that lies between our soul and our body with its ability to think, do, and speak. *That is, the thoughts, the words, and the body of a man have torn away from his soul by his sins, including the negative emotions.* Therefore, we are separated from God *by our own will*, for God is always in touch with the soul.

As I described in the chapter "Keep the Hearth of your Thoughts Pure!", the term "religion" comes from the word "religare", which translates from Latin as "restoring connection"; in this case, the Connection between man and God. Religion can take place when a denomination offers this bond. But if the denomination doesn't provide such Connection, then it has nothing to do with religion. It is safe to say that *not one* Christian denomination, cult, or any other spiritual practice on Earth is able to provide man with this bond, which they have proven with their helplessness. Look at what is happening in the world! Do you know a group of people or a nation that has really achieved this Connection through the Bible, including the Catholic or Protestant denominations? Do you know any Muslims who can offer this bond? Muslims have Shiites and Sunnis, which have further subdivisions and cults, including Muslim esoteric, such as Sufism. The same subdivisions are found in Judaism and Buddhism. So, in order to cease this separation, we need to link man with his soul, which results when we abolish our sins.

I have already explained how sins are eliminated: the old ones are destroyed with humility through acceptance of the Law for my punishment. There must be *real* acceptance with your soul, for the soul makes the man and not the brain. The brain is merely an instrument for our existence in the Material World. Next, the new sins must be reduced; and only then, the Heavens begin to brighten between you and your soul. And finally, man will manifest into the complete being.

Let me offer an illustration. The physical body is the most compact of man's possessions. The range of his ability to speak (the range of a sound) is broader than the body. For instance, a shout in the desert can be heard a kilometer away. A thought, or man's ability to think, has a much broader range than that of a sound. The ability to feel is even broader (Illustration 7). Next is the ability to perceive the ethereal and then animistic sensations, seeing such creatures as goblins and gnomes, which our ancestors were able to see. Those are real creatures, and they have specific names. Further, there is a spiritual intuitive perception, which is *the highest* perception we possess. The spirit does not dwell in the body; rather, the body exists within the spirit. The largest form we have is spiritual. Physical matter only encompasses all the galaxies and all the gross matter in general. However, we as spirits are far more expansive, and we carry enormous capabilities that we have lost because we blocked ourselves either through materialism or through some other faulty ideas: denominations, cults, esoteric teachings, and other pseudo-spiritual practices. Those are our walls, built by deceitful pastors, gurus, or by pseudoscience that does not accept God (Illustration 7). Again, we can break through those walls and restore the Connection only by eliminating the consequences of our downfall. This elimination happens only one way – obeying the Commandments.

11. BLIND FAITH

When Jesus came to Earth, He was the Line of Love from God. This was the last time reform was kindly offered to humanity, but people refused it. Jesus was murdered, and no one protected Him, not even his disciples: Judas betrayed Him, and Peter denied Him. Jesus said to Peter, "Before the rooster crows, you will disown Me three times." (Matthew, 26:34). Those were His "strong" disciples. Nevertheless, people made a lot of noise about the apostles. And perhaps the apostles were far better people than the rest of the crowd, but to proclaim them as saints or teachers who can deliver any kind of religion is *wrong*. Even Paul the apostle said, "For we know in part and we prophesy in part, but when completeness comes, what is in part disappears." (1 Corinthians, 13:9-11). "He has made us competent as ministers of a new covenant – not of the letter but of the Spirit; for the letter kills, but the Spirit gives life." (2 Corinthians, 3:6).

There are many passages in the Bible that don't make sense, including contradictions between the apostles. One says one thing, and the other says something different. And all of it is "laminated" and declared sacred. Anyone who questions it will be crossed out of the Book of Life! How convenient is that? Even Leo Tolstoy, after his research, said that when biblical texts were sorted and selected, the goal wasn't to find the Truth but to merge the Old Testament with the New Testament, having as few contradictions as possible. The task was successful to some extent. But the New Testament is an entirely different book.

You cannot take everything that was written *by people* who dubbed it the "Holy Book" and accept it as the full Truth. There are absolute inconsistencies in it, for example, where apostle Paul clearly contradicts apostle James. James writes in his message in the New Testament, "As the body without the Spirit is dead, so faith without deeds is dead." (James, 2:26). However, Paul states, "Know that a person is not justified by the works of the Law, but by faith in Jesus Christ." (Galatians, 2:16). Those two stands are in opposition to each other. Moreover, they contradict Christ, who said, "If you love Me, keep My Commands." "Love the Lord your God with all your heart and with all your soul and with all your mind. This is the first and greatest Commandment." (Matthew, 22:37-38). The Gospel of John, 14:15, states, "If you love Me keep My Commands." And later below it: "Anyone who does not love Me will not obey My teaching." (John, 14:24). Therefore, if you obey the Commandments, you are a Christian. If you do not obey them and don't even think of doing so, then you have nothing to do with Christianity! You might as well be a pagan, believing in nothing at all. I repeat His words: "So do not worry saying 'what shall we eat?' or 'what shall we drink?' or 'what shall we wear?' For the pagans run after all these things." (Matthew, 6:31-32). Aren't we pagans? Yes, we are. We fear what tomorrow might bring, and we search for what to eat and what to wear. We never look for the Kingdom of Heaven at all! *It is sought through our rectification.* Our correction requires absolutely precise instructions. How do we obtain them? We need to search and search tirelessly!

Along this process, people have joined different cults, esoteric groups, or churches. Those people came to me and said that they ran into situations where the teachers had no answer to some questions, or there would be no logic to their answers. When something doesn't fit and people start looking for the truth, those teachers will answer, "Who are you to argue with us? We are the priests, and you must listen to us." This amounts to an illogical mess. How can you grasp something that doesn't make sense?! A human is not a plant; we have a brain and a heart in order to understand things. Even Jesus Himself demanded *knowledge* and not simply blind faith: "If you hold to My teaching, you are really My disciples. Then you will <u>know</u> the truth, and the truth will set you free." (John, 8:31-32). *Know*, but not blindly believe in something! *This is God's <u>demand</u>!*

Blind faith is equivalent to ignorance and often leads to fanaticism. We need to obtain knowledge, not only so our souls can receive grace through faith, but also so our minds can understand the logic of Truth from the Creator. And such knowledge exists. Then the logic of the Light will conquer the logic of the Darkness, and intellect will serve man without degrading his soul, thereby fulfilling the Savior's Covenant: "Love the Lord your God with all your <u>heart</u> and with all your <u>soul</u> and with all your <u>mind</u>." (Matthew, 22:37). As a result of living by the Laws, we will become children of God and not the destroyers we are now. Aren't we now repeating the same mistakes of our two-thousand-year-old history? "Blind guides. If the blind lead the blind, both will fall into a pit." (Matthew, 15:14). Would it not be better to follow the phrase "Then you will know the truth, and the truth will set you free"? For now, freedom remains unseen.

We must *learn* about this world instead of blindly putting our faith in priests who don't truly believe in God themselves. If they believed in God, they would start living by the Laws. Instead, they justify themselves through the words of Paul, or Peter, or some other theologians, as if the Commandments are impossible to obey. So, on the one hand, they are saying, "You will burn in hell, you are the sinners, you have to obey the Commandments…" That is one side of their propaganda or preaching. What's the other side? As soon as you tell them, "Ok, I want to live by the Commandments, teach me!", to your great disappointment, you will find that a priest who has never made a step in the right direction cannot teach you a thing about it. He himself does not know how to do this! What can he teach a man? Nothing. We can learn to speak eloquently ourselves. Take a course on public speaking, and you will eventually become an exceptional speaker. You can speak with great expression, even better than those priests, but that doesn't mean the Commandments are being followed. Jesus also said, "Not everyone who says to Me 'Lord, Lord' will enter the Kingdom of Heaven, but only the one who does the will of My Father who is in Heaven." (Matthew, 7:21). And who does the Will of the Father, meaning who obeys the Commandments? No one. But somehow, all of the quotes of Christ are being ignored and instead, the quotes of the apostles are at the forefront. For instance, take Romans, 7:13 and all the way to the end. Paul is summarizing Christian religion: "We know that the law is spiritual, but I am unspiritual, sold as a slave to sin. I do not understand what I do. For what I want to do, I do not do, but what I hate I do. And if I do what I do not want to do, I agree that the law is good. As it is, it is no longer I myself who do it, but it is sin living in me. For I know that good itself does not dwell in me, that is, in my sinful nature. For I have the desire to do what is good, but I cannot carry it out. For I do not do the good I want to do, but the evil I do not want to do – this I keep on doing. Now if I do what I do not want to do, it is no longer I who do it, but it is sin living in me that does it." "So then, I myself in my mind am a slave to God's law, but in my sinful nature a slave to the law of sin." So, Paul acted like a patient from the psych ward. *He refused to hold his mind accountable for the deeds of his body.* I read it in amazement, thinking: how can this *nonsense* be offered to people as Christ's teaching?! It is the absolute opposite of the Truth. Paul did not even know Jesus in person. He knew *of* Him, but he wasn't His disciple. Paul preached a completely different religion – Judaism, which entered into a battle with Christ. They persecuted Christ, saying that if He ever came to Judea again, they would kill Him. Let's briefly recount the history of the Jewish people, so you understand what was happening before and at the time of Jesus, and on what basis it was happening.

When Moses realized that the Jewish people were not willing to obey the Commandments, he left them and then he died. I don't know under what circumstances he died. He broke the tablets, on which the same Ten Commandments were carved, and walked away, leaving the people with Jesus Navin. Jesus is a simple earthly name – Joshua. Jesus Navin was a follower of Moses, and he led the Jewish people to the Promised Land, which Moses had told them about. There they settled on both banks of the Jordan River, forming different tribes (Illustration 8). The two tribes of Issachar and Zebulun created the state of Galilee. Jesus was from Nazareth, the city of Galilee. That is why they called Him "the Galilean".

The state of Judah (Judea) was formed by Judas and Benjamin, the two tribes of Israel, and Jerusalem was here. At the community meeting of the people of Israel, Judah was declared the religious capital. There were also political capitals, and there was enmity between them. For instance, the tribe of Ephraim, which formed the state of Samaria, was in a quarrel with other tribes, because Ephraim was very proud and thus always at war. For that reason, it was said that there was nothing good ever to be expected out of Samaria.

But Jesus was not a Judean; He was an Israeli. In 937 B.C., the Jewish people were already divided politically. They no longer had one king, as Solomon and David were the last two kings. After that, the kingdom fell apart. Then came the concept of Israel and Judah. That is why not every Jew is a Judean. In Judah, there was the religion of Judaism, and Israel was left with the old Jewish religion. These two religions had discrepancies, which is why the fates of these two parts of the nation were completely different.

Bethlehem was within the territory of Judah. When there was a population census, and Mary came with Joseph to Bethlehem, Jesus was born. All hotels were full, and Jesus had to be born inside of a barn, laid to rest in a manger. This happened in Bethlehem. That is why it was described in the Old Testament that the Messiah would be born in Bethlehem, under the Star of Bethlehem, the Star of David. So, it happened, and Jesus was born in Bethlehem; but His parents' homeland was Nazareth. Following His birth, they were forced to flee Bethlehem, because the Magi told King

Herod that the King of Judah was born, who will end his supremacy. Because of this, King Herod ordered all infants born in Bethlehem that were less than two years of age to be killed. That was the Massacre of the Innocents. So, Mary and Joseph took Jesus and left Bethlehem for Egypt. Only after King Herod's death did they return to Nazareth (Matthew, 2).

Jesus grew up and started preaching at about 30 years of age. However, according to the chronology, King Herod died four years before the official birth of Christ. But the Massacre of the Innocents occurred during Herod's reign, which means we need to add another 2-3 years to Christ's age. Then it turns out that the real age of Jesus Christ is about seven years more. He was not 33 but 40 years old. This has already been proven but holds no significant value. It doesn't matter how old He was, because it is not important for understanding His sermons. Although, people often get carried away and start fighting over it, "No, your religion does not accept this, and ours does not accept that…" These things are *secondary*. The main idea – *His teaching* – was in the Commandments, His Sermon on the Mount, and His conversations with disciples.

Jesus came from Nazareth to preach in Judah, in Jerusalem, and was told that if He ever returned again, He would be killed. If we look back in history, we see that prior to the coming of Christ, the wrong religion mostly came out of Judah. The wars started happening and Israel, the north, was brought under Assyria, and the south, a little later, under Babylon. They had different fates, different captivity. Following Babylon, Judah was conquered by King Cyrus, and then by the Romans. Then again, the wailing started due to constant captivity, genocide, the extermination of the best population, and terrible humiliation. And again came the cry, "God, help us!" God heard them once more because they were the first of the monotheistic nations. They were no longer pagans; they attracted Moses as monotheists because they were a spiritually advanced nation. It is fruitless to send God to pagans because He won't be understood. By the Law of Resemblance, those nations gravitate to God, whose consciousness has grown to monotheism. So, God heard them and sent His Highest Power. But due to the deeply rooted religious misconceptions of the region, Jesus came upon great opposition to His teaching in Judah. Thus, He went to Judah, knowing He would be killed. That is a bit of history to aid your understanding of the development of events.

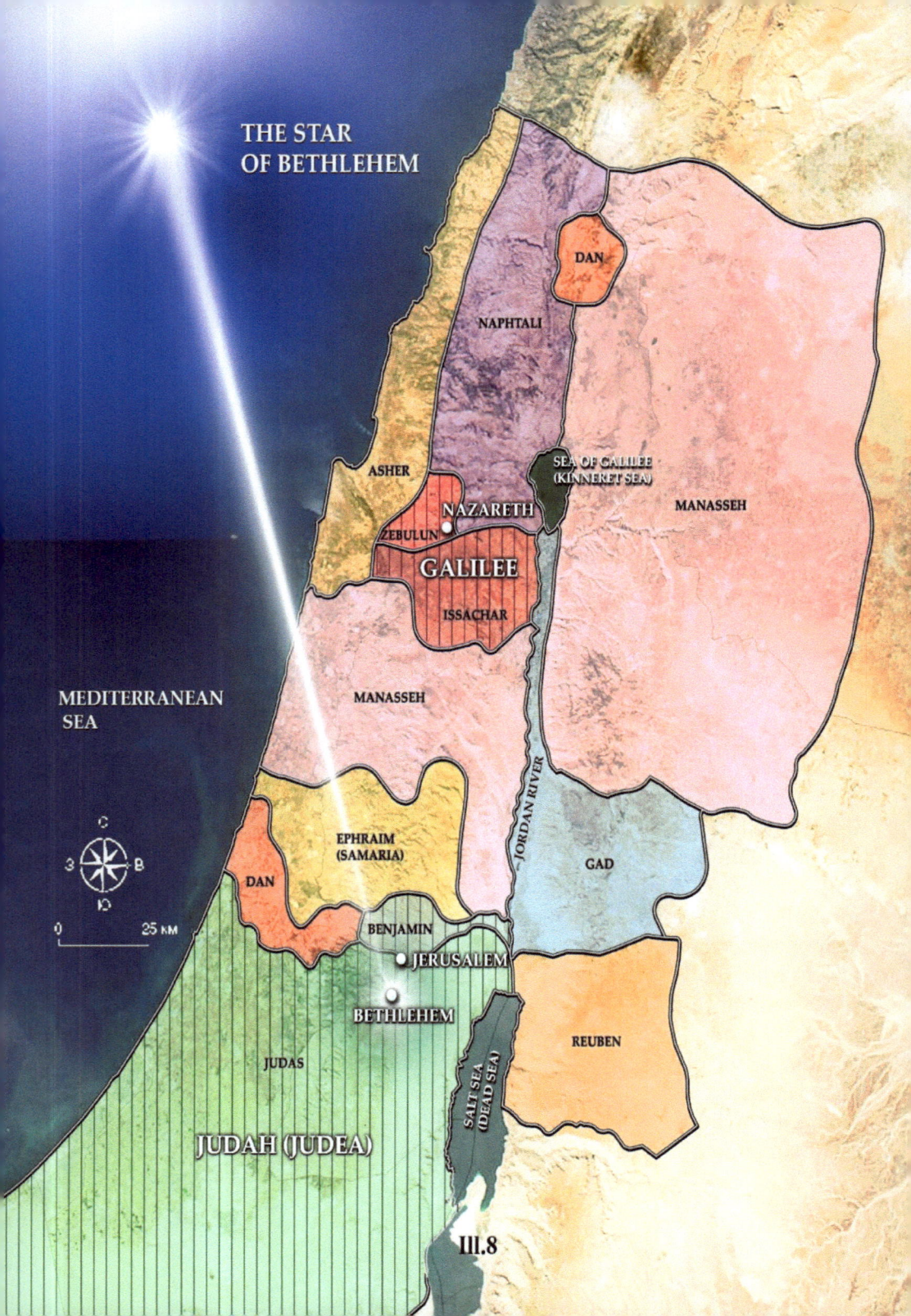

THE STAR
OF BETHLEHEM

DAN

NAPHTALI

ASHER

SEA OF GALILEE
(KINNERET SEA)

MANASSEH

NAZARETH

ZEBULUN

GALILEE

ISSACHAR

MEDITERRANEAN
SEA

MANASSEH

JORDAN RIVER

N

W   E

S

0   25 KM

DAN

EPHRAIM
(SAMARIA)

GAD

BENJAMIN

JERUSALEM

BETHLEHEM

JUDAS

REUBEN

SALT SEA
(DEAD SEA)

JUDAH (JUDEA)

III.8

Judah wasn't the only place Jesus was not accepted. Surprisingly, Christ's parents and siblings rebuked Him for carrying out His teachings rather than taking care of the family. They thought that since He was the eldest son, it was His job to look after them. But Jesus came for the entire Earth, and the scope of His work encompassed all the people of Earth. His abilities were immense. He performed miracles, but His relatives were trying to stop Him from teaching and instead keep Him as their pocket assistant. So, Jesus' family did not support Him in His work. That is when Jesus said, "Truly I tell you no prophet is accepted in his hometown." (Luke, 4:24).

Nevertheless, Mary was deified and sculpted into the Mother of God. That took place through the course of several ecumenical councils. Historically, those who refused to support the concept of "Mary the Mother of God" were killed. In reality, Mary was Jesus' *earthly* mother who gave Him a physical body as a vessel for His presence on Earth. That was her mission. But to announce her saint or divine, turning her into a subject of worship, is wrong. Jesus' words are a testimony to that. "Now Jesus' mother and brothers came to see Him, but they were not able to get near Him because of the crowd. Someone told Him, 'Your mother and brothers are standing outside, wanting to see you.' He replied, 'My mother and brothers are those who hear God's word and put it into practice'." (Luke, 8:19-21).

12. PSEUDO-CHRISTIANITY

To help people realize their mistakes and abandon the erroneous path leading to destruction, humanity has received help from Above since the beginning of time. Krishna, Zoroaster, and Moses came from the World of Primordial Spirits, and Jesus Christ came from God (Illustration 5). They all preached the same thing: live by the Commandments, follow the Commandments, obey the Commandments! But the greedy crowd of Pharisees and teachers of all kinds quickly gathered around this notion and started creating lies. *That is why not one religious idea _fully_ became the property of our souls!* We feel something good from the Church: there are good appeals, and often, there are good people. Unfortunately, certain dogmas have killed Christian religion. Which ones? Blood sacrifice as atonement for all sins, which is the *core* dogma of all Christian religions. ***Jesus Christ never redeemed anything with His blood. HE NEVER REDEEMED ANYTHING!***

In their enormous vanity, people imagined that they are so important to God, that God would send His own Son to slaughter. Where is the justice? People will commit horrible evils, and God will come to Earth and perish because of them. As a reward, they'll nail Him to the cross and say, "It is so sickening here, You should come more often. The more often, the better! We will destroy you again and go on with our lives, feeling all better and atoned for our sins." That's the nonsense people have come up with.

For the sake of argument, let's approach from the contrary and assume that Jesus did redeem our sins. In that case, why do we, who believe in Christ, continue to suffer? WHY?! Thus, this alone already speaks of lies. *The world is not corrected by mere faith in Christ* like apostle Paul once asserted, "Know that a person is not justified by the works of the Law, but by faith in Jesus Christ." (Galatians, 2:16). According to Paul, only faith saves and redeems all sins; we cannot redeem our sins. "For we maintain that a person is justified by faith apart from the works of the law." (Romans, 3:28). And only Jesus, our ransom for sin, washes it all off with His blood: "…and all are justified freely by His grace through the redemption that came by Jesus Christ. God presented Christ as a sacrifice of atonement, through the shedding of His blood – to be received by faith. He did this to demonstrate His righteousness because in His forbearance He had left the sins committed beforehand unpunished." (Romans, 3:24-25). Surprisingly, we do not feel as though our sins are washed away. I am not speaking of the non-believers, but about the ones who do believe. There are so many older people who sincerely believe, but in reality, their faith is fallacious.

There is a book that accurately arranges all the accents – *In the Light of Truth* by Oskar Ernst Bernhardt (Abd-Ru-Shin). The author writes that those are *false* paths, led by *false* faith. *The true faith pushes people to strive to become better*. Just think about it: if I truly and sincerely believe in God with all my heart and soul, what right do I have to live outside the Law?! If I believe in God the Creator, His presence and the absolute perfection, and that He demands the same perfection from me, then how can I believe and yet not follow the Law? It is absurd! It is the hypocrisy: I believe in God, but I don't care about the Laws. Perhaps people do not openly say this, but they sure act that way. And it doesn't matter whether we know the Laws or not, as we have all heard of this applicable legal principle: ignorance of law does not absolve you of responsibility. That is why life beats us down daily, yet we cannot figure out the reason.

You won't find a single quote by Jesus Christ to the effect of "It's impossible to be sinless; therefore, I redeem your sins with My death, to abolish your responsibility over them." If that were the case, this notion would be repeated consistently by all authors of the Gospels. For it is the most crucial element of religion! Instead, that notion contradicts the Law of the Father: "A man reaps what he sows" (Galatians, 6:7). *This means that the officially accepted dogma that our sins are redeemed by the blood of the murdered Christ <u>does not coincide</u> with God's Law of personal responsibility for one's own actions.* Moreover, it indirectly indicates that God gave man the impossible task of personally redeeming our sins while living by the Commandments.

In reality, Jesus suggested something completely different from this sacrilegious option proclaimed by Paul the apostle. Salvation, He says, is in the fulfillment of His Word! I am reminding you of Christianity: Matthew, 22:36. Christ's answer to the question "Which is the greatest Commandment in the Law?" was "Love the Lord your God with all your heart and with all your soul and with all your mind. This is the first and greatest Commandment." What does it mean "to love God"? The Gospel of John states, "If you love Me, keep My Commands." "Anyone who loves Me will obey My teaching." "Anyone who does not love Me will not obey

My teaching." *That is the entirety of Christianity!* The rest is just the development of this matter from different angles: parables, conversations with students, and the like. But suddenly, the apostles say something different. So the apostles aren't Christians and carry non-Christian motives. If you want to be a Christian, act according to Christ and not according to the apostles!

Many might ask, "If blood sacrifice wasn't an intended part of Christ's Mission, then why did God not prevent the death of His Son?"

Everyone, including Jesus Christ, falls under the Law of Choice, and God does not change His Laws. A Visitor, when coming to Earth, voluntarily accepts all possible consequences, including physical death. *That is what constitutes the grandeur of the heroic act of Jesus Christ!* Humanity, to whom the Son of God addressed His Message, could have chosen to embrace It. People could have decided to follow Christ and to become the nation led by God. But the supreme spiritual authority of that time did not want to admit its inadequacy. The massacre of the Savior was bolstered by fanaticism or indifference of the masses. "The blind leading the blind" chose to murder! After the torture and execution of Jesus Christ, all that remains is to wait for the Last Judgement as an extreme measure. *Humanity rejected the real opportunity to be saved and confirmed its intentions by nailing the Savior to the cross.*

Jesus came and created a religion of Light on Earth. He gave us the Light, which is living by the Commandments! The twelve apostles fragmented Christ's teaching into different directions. Judas hung himself, but then another apostle came along, meaning they split into twelve disparate parts. They began to create their own religion based on their personal misinterpretations of the teaching of Christ. Their vanity was not defeated. They spoke of Christ as a great figure, of salvation, of living by His Word, and on and on! People wondered, "What did He say? How do we interpret His phrases?" And the apostles gave their opinions. Not being particularly astute, they began to distort the pure teaching. Then the twelve religions were born. The generation passed. Decades passed after Christ's death. Each of the apostles had their own disciples, the interpreters, and then they had their own, so the tree began to branch further. To date, we are dealing with anywhere from six hundred to several thousand Christian religions and cults. And that's only the Christian factions! Therefore, the system of delusion is enormous.

Being ignorant in the matters of religion, we have entrusted all this knowledge and research to priests. And you see what they have done. But don't blame them. Once again, they are guilty of their laziness, and we of ours. We believed them for centuries without trying to understand these imperative matters of religion. We were too lazy to realize that obeying the Commandments is, in fact, what solves *all* of our earthly problems. However, one must be *actively working* on their character, instead of gazing at the pedestals of saints, thinking how difficult it must be, and how they would rather go their own way, even if it's a sinful path. That is how one quits before this Mountain, which in the Bible is called Mount Zion, strange as it may seem.

In the chapter "Revelation" of the New Testament, Jesus conveyed to John the theologian that on Mount Zion there will be 144,000 righteous ones, with the Lamb at the head. They will be saved. "Then I looked, and there before me was the Lamb, standing on Mount Zion, and with Him 144,000 who had His name and His Father's name written on their foreheads." (Revelation, 14:1). Mount Zion? That *is* what we are climbing! Mount Zion isn't a man-made mountain. It is, metaphorically speaking, the meadows of alpine purity where the soul is pure. And one can climb that Mount anywhere: in Tashkent, Beijing, Moscow, New York, in the suburbs, or even in your own vegetable garden. The main thing is *to actually climb!* These people will be on Mount Zion; thus, they are the real "Zionists". They are the ones climbing that Mountain *by amending themselves.* And the ones who aren't climbing are looking for some landmark where Moses once was. The legend is: if you climb to the top and spend the night there, all your sins will be gone. What kind of nonsense is that?! Surprisingly, people believe in it.

Satan knows very well our leading quality – spiritual laziness; and he appeases it with various similar concepts. As humans, we are ravenous to receive everything for free. Go and obtain absolution immediately. Get on your knees and climb the holy stairs (the Scala Sancta) in Rome, and so on.

I recently watched a documentary about Girolamo Savonarola, who voiced his opinion on the topic of such a mode of redemption from sin. He said something to the effect of, "Is it really that simple? Some scoundrel will climb the stairs on his knees, and everything will be forgiven to him? I disagree." He voiced his opposition, and they burned him, just like they burned others. Throughout history, the Church was a source of violence and battle against people who genuinely tried to understand the system of religion. Jan Hus and Jerome of Prague were burned - two theologians and decent people, who did not even offer any reforms. They simply addressed the priests with the request to make an effort to set a good example for the congregation because people were already making jokes about their gluttony and other vices. Half of the jokes in medieval times were about the Popes, which they deserved. All that Jan Hus offered was to set an example. He didn't even try to understand the essence of Christ's religion. So, he was stamped out with the words "Who are you to teach us?! Burn him!" And they did. Such was the brethren – can't argue with it. There are so many sins recorded after them – in the name of God they would take hundreds of thousands of people and burn, torture, put them through inquisitions, you name it, while hypocritically proclaiming Christianity as the religion of repentance, mercy, and all-forgiveness. What kind of Christianity is that?! I remember the movie *Kingdom of Heaven* about Jerusalem. They showed the crusades - killing, killing, and killing. A few naïve people thought that by taking Jerusalem from the Saracens, the Muslims, they would start serving God. Nothing of the sort. All that the knights showed was an enormous thirst for profit, power, and realization of their foolishness. Those who tried any different were killed. That's the history of the bloody crusades. Those were the people who called themselves "the Christians".

So, there was always an ongoing battle of the clergy against the Truth, which is why no Messenger ever appeared in the body of a priest. Jesus was the son of a carpenter, not the son of a Rabbi. Zoroaster was the son of a shepherd. There has never been a Prophet in the body of a priest anywhere on Earth. Wouldn't that be great?! Let's put this charge of Light into the Roman Pope! He would tell everyone the truth, starting with *repentance*, as we burned so many people who stood in pursuit of the Truth. So, we must repent and begin to live by the Commandments. But if he dared to voice that in his surroundings, the cardinals would most certainly stab him, bury his words, and continue with their own because they are always working against the Truth. In fact, the Christian church is a *pseudo-Christian* church, whether it's the Catholic version, the variants of Protestantism, or Orthodoxy.

The Orthodoxy alone has six directions. There are 2-3 thousand different directions of Protestants. That's only the directions! There are about

1.2 billion Catholics against 260 million Orthodox and maybe 800 million Protestants. In sum, we have approximately 2.26 billion Christians on Earth. There are about 1 billion Muslims. If we add Buddhists and Jews, there are 4 billion "believers". But if you notice, the most advanced and developed Christian, Muslim, and Jewish countries bring the most harm upon the Earth. It's not the pagans, Chukchi, the aborigines of Australia, or some other barely rising nations causing harm. No. These nations might be harming themselves with their ignorance and underdevelopment. But those religious countries destroy other countries, subordinating them to their interests. What kind of *"religion"* is this?! Deceiving your neighbor, your own fellow citizen, or another country through ugly diplomacy or threats, is considered a tremendous success. Those are the people of the Earth! The people born by the Light in spirit! Of course, God has to stop this whole business. "When" is only a matter of time. Obviously, the end is coming. God will no longer tolerate this behavior, as He is the Master of this Creation. *Either you live by the Law or be destroyed like the weeds. This process has begun.*

13. ON THE EVE

In recent years, after observing what is happening in society and nature, many conclude that the apogee of the final Judgement is rapidly approaching. The separation of "sheep" from "goats" is taking place. The majority of people who pay attention to global developments cannot deny the fact that the situation on the planet is *especially bad* now. Why? Currently, it is an unusual time on Earth. Before, there was a laminar development of events, more gradual: what a man sowed, that was he reaping, i.e., *slowly* sowing and reaping. Years would pass, even decades between crime and punishment, whereas now that time is very quickly shrinking. The terms are changing, and the acceleration is happening. Catastrophes are increasing on the planet. All of this means that God has *forcibly* turned on the mechanism of suppressing all evil on Earth. And not only evil itself, but its main carriers - people!

One cannot accuse Satan of being the evil we see in the world. He is a false beginning. *Lucifer pushes people to do evil but never forces!* The evil we do is our ultimate choice.

Not one of you can say that Satan ever forced you to be rude to someone or to hurt anyone. That has never happened. You can choose to restrain yourself or not, depending on your patience and willpower. You may or may not choose to act correctly in *any* situation. For example, some people have decided that everything is free to be stolen. So, if I work at a factory, I could steal some parts and sell them. Or I could take and sell medicine and profit from it, and so on. Some people think this is normal. Others feel that selling liquor and cigarettes is normal, or that manufacturing them is considered honest labor. However, honest money is made through honest labor that is directed towards the benefit of society and not at its destruction and debauchery.

Despite all this, there is no need to hate bad people, be angry with them, or even resent them. *Forgive them!* They will answer to God, for God is the Creator, and He never forgets anything. The recording is on, and in due time it will happen. Don't hurry God by saying "God, can't You see what is happening?!" He does see, and, when necessary, everything will be done just right.

One day the pushing pressure coming from the herders (Illustration 6) will stop. In the Bible, those people are referred to as "the wolves", and the ordinary people are "the sheep" (John, 10:12). So, when the wolves gnaw the sheep, the sheep will either enter under the Law or fall under the attack of the wolves. *You* make that choice! This pressure will eventually reach everyone: one will be reached this month, another one in six months, and the third one in a year. This battering is happening to everybody, and, one by one, people are losing the battle. *The peak moment has arrived for all of us!*

As soon as God decides that there has been enough of that pressure, this process will come to an end. Then, those who came under the Law will be protected by It, and those who did not will be crushed by the Evil. Meaning, *the greater evil will destroy the lesser evil.* And then the Evil itself will fall under the blows of the Creator. The Law will obliterate it! This process is what is referred to as the Apocalypse, the famous biblical "Revelation". John wrote about it, describing the circumstances of the events. It is also written using more modern language in the three-volume book of Oscar Ernst Bernhardt, *In the Light of Truth*. In fact, this book is the Gospel promised by Jesus.

14. THE FINAL GOSPEL

The word "Gospel" means "the good news". When Jesus left, there were attempts to reproduce His words with some degree of accuracy. They called it the Gospel of Christ, the New Testament. Jesus Christ said that before the end of the ages, there would be many developments: hunger and disease, earthquakes and floods, wars, and the rumors of wars, meaning *the turmoil will accrue*. All this was happening before, only not in such quantity. Now it is increasing each year. "Because of the increase of wickedness, the love of most will grow cold" (Matthew, 24:12). People already *openly* don't love each other; only a few have some sort of warm feelings for one another. In reality, nations fear each other, and people, in general, are afraid of one another for good reason. We already live in a world where children deceive their parents and even murder them for money and property. Many horrible things take place; it is true turmoil. And the "island" of normal people is shrinking in size because they fall under the blows of the bad ones, or they get into some valueless pseudo-spiritual teachings that don't provide any help.

Predicting this turmoil, Jesus spoke, "All these are the beginning of birth pains" (Matthew, 24:8). He also spoke that later *another* Gospel of the Kingdom will come and will be preached to all nations. Then the end will come "…but the one who stands firm to the end will be saved. And this gospel of the Kingdom will be preached in the whole world as a testimony to all nations, and then the end will come." (Matthew,24:13-14). Christian denominations attribute these words to the Bible, explaining to their congregation that the Gospel Jesus talked about is the Bible, which is being preached throughout the world. *However, it is not so.* Jesus was referring to a different Gospel, and it has arrived. Thus, the appearance of the book *In the Light of Truth*, the Gospel promised by Jesus, is one of the last omens.

The book was officially published in my country in the 90s, but years prior, it came out in underground publishing. However, back then, no one took much interest in it. Now, it is being published in many languages throughout the world. It is a very unusual book. I first came across it in November of 1995. A woman brought me the book at the end of my first class and said, "You are teaching just like it's written in this book." I was surprised to hear her words. As much as I had encountered esotericism, I always felt there was something off. So, I decided to check it out. I took the book and felt joy radiating from it. Somehow, I knew that it was my book. I just had a very good feeling. I had already developed a pretty good intuitive perception by then, which is the most accurate gauge we possess. Our brain is only equipped with logic. It can draw conclusions and make decisions based on logical reasoning. For us to make an accurate conclusion about a book, we must first read it, perceive it, and evaluate it correctly. Unfortunately, our brain is often led by some false ideas and is *unable* to give an accurate evaluation. For that, everyone will ignore this book to some extent. And only your soul, equipped with this gauge of the intuitive perception, can sense the goodness radiating from it, the boundless joy. I had already developed that gauge by then.

I'll rewind in time and say that within the first few days of working on myself, I received a warning. By then, I had already begun to tackle irritability and the feeling of being offended. I conquered jealousy rather fast, and my fear died within a month. When these changes started happening, I thought to myself, "It seems that I am trying to live by the Commandments. Maybe I need to read the Bible…" And I was told, "It is too early for you to read the Bible, for you won't be able to discern what is from God and what is from man. You don't have enough determining power through your own radiation, meaning you are still too deep in your sins. The time will come, and you will sense that you are ready to understand what is in the Bible from God and what is from man. Leave it alone for now. Otherwise, you will simply become one of the thousands of interpreters throughout history." I felt there was truth to this. So, I started changing. Only about two years later and after reading *In the Light of Truth* did I begin to sense the Bible.

In the Light of Truth describes everything we need to know, including how people came to false faith and many other details. When I started reading, it took me a few months to fully comprehend; I realized that it contained identical information to what I'd already been receiving. Everything came together like a jigsaw puzzle! Then I finally felt at peace. Because the first two years of going it alone against everyone were pretty hard. The human psyche is used to certain collectivism. I thought that just one person couldn't be right where the rest are wrong: all churches, cults, esoteric groups, all materialists are wrong, and only I am right. I was always tormented by it. I thought it was impossible for only one person to be right. I thought that I was challenged by vanity. But when this book arrived, along with my future experience, I realized – yes, I was right. I understood then the words of Jesus, who was also alone against everybody. He said to His disciples, "If the world hates you, keep in mind that it hated Me first." (John, 15:18). Because He exposed that its deeds are evil. Of course, the world will hate you when you reveal all of its lies: here is the Orthodox lie, the Catholic lie, the Theosophy lie, the Steiner's anthroposophy, Krishnaism, and false *Bhagavat Gita*, and so on. I find lies in those pages and say, "Look at what you and your leaders are writing; this is absurd!" And they start shaking with anger because I exposed them, just like a snake that bites when cornered. That's how one by one those false idols fall.

The same way Jesus Christ came and uncrowned them one after another. But He was God. If you follow Him, you unknowingly put on that "harness" and experience, to some extent, everything He did – the pressure and harassment from those who oppose His teaching. And when you come out beyond physical matter, the astral battle begins. The whole lie of this world tries to knock you over. How can one man alone withstand all the evil of this world? *Without the help of God's Will, he cannot.* Thus, my "corridor" is being held by the Holy Spirit, and I keep going *with Its help and only so*. That is why I don't consider my spiritual growth and all the changes to be solely my achievements. One can demonstrate will and patience, but he is nothing here without God, at least not now.

There were times when one could break through by himself, but those times are long gone. There were no Prophets back then. But after we blocked ourselves entirely with our sins, the intermediaries became needed, who came and pulled us by our ears with their knowledge and power. That is what's taking place now. Of course, I asked myself and people have asked me, "Who are you?" One person called me a combination of a super magician and psychic mixed with Christianity and something else... Finally, one journalist asked me, "What do you consider yourself?" I said, "A human who is on the path of earning this title – 'human'."

Indeed, the title of "human" sounds proudly, but it must be earned. We are the seeds planted in this soil, and we must learn to live by human laws which equal spiritual laws. The word "human" translates from Sanskrit as "eternal spirit". So, I will become human only after I learn to live by God's Laws, which are the Commandments. And that is holiness. *Then* I will have earned the right to call myself a *human*. If I was unlawful, ignorant, and lazy in spirit, and I started getting rid of my laziness while learning the

Laws of my Creator, I thus began to acquire knowledge, lose my ignorance, and understand the blessing of living by the Laws. I slowly become a "human", and I need no other title. I'm not a psychic with super abilities and super qualities. What is *super*? We are merely restoring *our natural quality*. It is *necessary*, and there should be no vanity in it. If a criminal is rectifying himself and transforming from a villain into a decent man, what is so super about that? *That is my duty as a human!* I don't want to cause any harm. I genuinely want to stop harming this world, and thus the Laws stop harming me with retribution. Such reciprocity has already been proven by the experiences of many dozens of people. The difference is that I am a little stronger; thus, I protect many people who are on this road. When they encounter problems, I help them.

After reading *In the Light of Truth*, I realized that this is the Gospel. Hundreds of thousands of people recognize it outside of my input. Those who read it are stunned by its power! Only it should be read not just with your intellect, but also with your soul. When you involve your soul, you can understand this book very well. If you read it with your brain only, this book becomes quite heavy. The author explains that this book is a semi-finished product. It enables you to work. The text is seemingly simple, but it's quite difficult to absorb. To understand each paragraph, you must dig into it, picturing the imagery. Only then do you begin to comprehend the essence. But you'll grasp it only on a minor level at first.

I read it for the first time in 1995. After a month, I felt as though I had never even read the book. I was drawn back to it. It was as if I was reading phrases I had never seen before! They were new to me. I started comprehending them on a whole new level. Because before I read it, my consciousness was trifling. After I read it, my consciousness expanded. There was a lot that I began to realize. The next time I read it, my consciousness was able to better understand it because of this expansion. I was able to absorb and penetrate the text better. So, each time I read it, it gives me the expansion of consciousness. No matter how many times you read it, you'll continue to expand. Others have the same experience – it gives them something new each time they read it! When you run into a difficult life situation, and you need answers, I say, "Don't forget, you have another helper besides me - the book!" One opens the book on precisely the page that explains what they are looking for. It works every time, one hundred percent! Why? Because this is the Gospel. It makes sure you open to exactly where you need. It has happened to me many times already.

So, in reading the book, I thought no man could write like that! I felt that this book was too profound to be written by an ordinary man. Who wrote this book?! The answer came to me five years later. I received the following information: the man who wrote this book came previously as John the Baptist, and before that, he came as Elijah the Prophet. If anyone knows a little of the Bible, they remember that the same individual first appeared as Elijah the Prophet and later again as John the Baptist. Jesus confirmed it Himself: "The disciples asked Him, 'Why do the teachers of the Law say that Elijah must come first?' Jesus replied, 'To be sure, Elijah comes and will restore all things. But I tell you, Elijah has come, and they did not recognize him, but have done to him everything they wished'" (Matthew, 17:10-12), referring to John the Baptist. So first, there was Elijah the Prophet, then the same person came as John the Baptist, and later again as the writer Oscar Ernest Bernhardt. This is the same Prophet. He always precedes major events. Just like John the Baptist, who baptized Jesus, said, "He is the one who comes after me, the strap of whose sandals I am not worthy to untie." (John, 1:27). "A man who comes after me has surpassed me because He was before me. I myself did not know Him, but the reason I came baptizing with water was that He might be revealed to Israel." (John, 1:30-31).

Now the same person came again and said that the Son of Man is coming, bringing the Final Judgment. Take the Bible, Matthew, chapters 24 and 25, and it is written where Jesus states that when the Son of Man appears, there will be Judgment. "As it was in the days of Noah, so it will be at the coming of the Son of Man." (Matthew, 24:37). ***The Son of Man and the Son of God are two different figures***, unlike the way it has been presented to us by the Church.

15. PROPHETS,
THE SON OF GOD, THE SON OF MAN

Man came to Earth in order to overcome his spiritual laziness by surviving in the dense matter of the Physical World. He must learn this world through personal experience. *He must learn* and not blindly believe without understanding! ***Man must come into the Spiritual World consciously!***

Today, not one theory or teaching, except the teaching of Jesus Christ, is able to pull a person out of the swamp of sin and lead them to spiritual ascension. Why is Jesus Christ, in my opinion, the best guide into the Spiritual World? Because Jesus was God, and the rest were Prophets. Before Christ, there was Moses. He was also a Prophet from God. But over 3000 years, his Laws were badly distorted. Jesus's teaching has been distorted for 2000 years. But, unlike Moses, Jesus was of the Creator. Thus, the physics of His abilities were much greater. "Physics" from Greek is "nature". His nature of the Creator doesn't equal the nature of the created beings, even the Prophets.

I have a mechanical education, so I'll draw a parallel to explain. Let's assume the "pull" of the Prophets is one ton, then the pull of Jesus has no limits. There will be as much effort as necessary to pull you out of the swamp of sin. The only condition is *you must want it*. Then you will be pulled out like a carrot from a garden bed. Yes, it will hurt stripping away your sins, but you will be pulled out! *Redemption is always painful.*

Due to the thick density of the Astral World, the Prophet's strength isn't enough now. The theory is the same - fulfill the Commandments, but only the Creator has enough power. The Creator would have never sent His Highest Element of help if it wasn't absolutely necessary, because the Creator is Perfection! And Perfection never does anything superfluous. He chooses the exact techniques and exact dosage of what's needed at the moment on Earth and in the Creation. There is perfection in that!

First, He sent the *created beings*, then the *primordial beings*, and finally, *He Himself* came. The scale of the intermediaries was changing.

At first, a long time ago, the Astral World was covered by only a slight haze of our sins. The closer to our time, the denser the sins became. And by the time of Christ's coming, it became much more difficult to break this already condensed barrier. Thus, a long time ago, liberated spirits from our class could cope with the task. After that, the primordial beings, the Prophets, came to the rescue. And when the layer of sins became too thick, they said, "God, we cannot cope anymore! The density of evil is too great." That's why Jesus Himself came and died here. Human consciousness failed without realizing that He was *the only* way out. They didn't protect the Helper. Thus, the Earth immersed into the darkness again.

After the murder of Christ, from the Highest Authority it was recognized that it is *useless* to communicate with Earth through the intermediaries! Because people either chase them away or kill them. Then what? What other option does Perfection have? You have been given many years for amendment. If you aren't willing, the Judgment will come. If you ask *when* the end will be, let's turn to Matthew, chapter 24, again. The disciples asked: when will be "the end of the age" and the Second Coming? The answer was: when famine and disease intensify. They have always existed, but they will *increase!* Famine, disease, wars, and hatred towards each other will grow. When earthquakes, floods, and wars increase, the end will come. But that's only the beginning. There will be the Gospel of Kingdom, and *then* the end will come. Again, the promised Gospel is the book *In the Light of Truth*. "But the one who stands firm to the end will be saved." (Matthew, 24:13). Those saved will be the ones who don't steal or do other adversities. They endure with their soul and call for God, "God, help! It is unbearable to live! What's next? Help!" And the help is sent. It came, and now the Word sounds on Earth. *Take It and use It!* **Make the Word your way of life!** But one must distinguish where the Word of Truth is and where the liars mask themselves as "the Truth".

God created the human spirit. And we create forms, for we were granted that ability. The human spirit has specific properties – it attracts. We attract everything. In order not to attract something horrible, we are given *desire*. Desire is the selectivity of attraction; it is its base. Let's say I want something salty, or I want to listen to music, or to sit in the park and listen to the sound of the falling leaves or the murmur of the brook. Or I want to be active, to run around. This is what I want. This is my wish! So, the wish is born, and I go and do it. The same way attraction is formed.

If a person wants something good for himself, love and happiness, he starts seriously searching for a way to achieve that. In the process, he finds some apathetic options and even sees that they are lacking, but nevertheless, he succumbs to the comforting idea of being a part of the great Orthodox Church, for example. Whom else will he listen to when the Church carries great authority? And those speaking to him about the Commandments have no such authority. Who is his navigator? One must choose for himself. The majority would rather remain in the bosom of the Orthodox Church. It's more comfortable. This way, one can slowly rot for a long time. But otherwise, you must fight! Shake yourself out, get yourself together, and make yourself work! It is hard! Thus, people justify their laziness with false authorities. To do so is their right. *We choose!* It all depends on our choice.

If one chooses a Prophet, he can start going. But he will encounter obstacles the Prophet *cannot* help to overcome with his power of radiation. The Prophets could have provided that help 2, 3, 5 thousand years ago. But now, due to the changing situation that is the greatly increased density of our sins, it is impossible! The prophetic forces are unable to break you through, despite all their truth. They have only the physics of the *created*, which is limited. But God carries *boundless* possibility. I repeat it: apart from Christianity, *nothing* on Earth can pull a person out! Once again - the lifting force is great. Thus, to break through from where we are, I rely on Infinity. Then I have a chance. If I rely only on Prophets, there is not enough lifting force to even clear away the "chaff". It is impossible due to their limited potential. Thus, there is a rational grain to why I have chosen precisely the Highest Authority.

There are no national Prophets or God's Messengers. Those who came did not have national coloring. They come to work for the entire Earth. People who appropriate a Prophet are wrong. A Prophet is the property of the Earth, and so is his Word! It always was and still remains.

Jesus once said that another advocate would come - the Spirit of Truth, which is *another* Line, different from that of Jesus'. The Spirit who comes is unlike the Son of God. The Son of God came and wasn't connected with anything else but God. That is, the Unsubstantiated Core of God came to Earth, clad in all cloaks of the levels of the Creation, including the earthly cloak of Jesus from Nazareth. Jesus is an earthly name, a simple Jewish name. It could have been any other name. And Christ is translated as "the Savior"; He will save people from their sins. With what? Well, not with His blood! *But with His Word!*

So, Jesus won't come, but the Other One will, along the Trinity Line - the Spirit of Truth. Jesus was the Son, and the Second One is the Spirit, *God as the Spirit.*

What comprises a Trinity? God is one, but He expresses Himself in different ways. In order to understand the essence of the Trinity, we can compare it very remotely with what we know of man, although it is an entirely different concept.

Suppose I can do one thing with one hand, another thing with another hand while thinking about a third thing. That means I have a certain degree of freedom. I often give the following example because it was an experience I had when my child was very small, and my wife asked me to make some porridge. Back then, I was studying at a university. I was reading a book while making porridge. So, I turned on the autopilot of stirring the pot. That way, I didn't have to worry about it anymore. I was stirring while reading my study material. At the same time, my cat started rubbing up against my leg, and I pushed it away. Do you see how many different movements I have made? One hand was stirring, another one was holding the book, my brain was reading and comprehending, and my leg was pushing the cat. If a man can do so many things at the same time, how can we deny God of having a much higher degree of freedom?

Thus, His right hand is Love, and the left hand is Will. The right hand came to Earth in a physical body, but the body was not God. People from other religions quite reasonably reproach, including in the Koran, that we have many Gods: "There is God, and Jesus is God too?" But the body was not God. *The body was the instrument for delivering knowledge.* In order to convey the Truth to people who were under the blockade of the lie, it was necessary to break through this blockade. For that, God was sent in the human body. That human body had not only to learn the language of the nation but to find out the root causes of the lie, meaning to learn the entire system of erroneous human beliefs, and say, "This all is not the Truth! Look, there is no logic here, here, and here. All you speak is a lie. And *this* is the real religion!" And that religion had to be presented to the people. How can one do this without having a tongue or a brain? It is impossible! Because people lost revelation. Humans have lost the ability of their brain to connect with the Light and receive information on the mental level because any waves coming from Above were distorted by erroneous human consciousness and by the priests. Any person who didn't listen to the priests was killed, cursed out, anathematized, and so on. Priests carried out a very harsh regime, giving no freedom in any knowledge. One had to blindly believe in what *they* were offering, *those who did not obey the Commandments themselves!*

The Son of God, during His life on Earth, already knew that people would fail. He saw our weaknesses, manifested in the people He interacted with. Thus, He proclaimed His prediction of the Second Messenger. Why would we need the Second Coming if at least one of the denominations were following the right path to the Light? If that were the case, the congregation would learn by the example of their spiritually experienced priests. Then, people would be taught how to obey the Commandments, which would result in the gradual improvement of their spiritual and physical lives. Consequently, such people would become an example to follow. That is the inevitable outcome of living by the Laws of the Creator. The opposite of that would be the devastation, disease, and humiliation that serve as punishment for our sins.

So, Jesus said before He died that He was going away, and the world would not see Him again. "And I will ask the Father, and He will give you another advocate to help you and be with you forever – the Spirit of truth." (John, 14:16-17). God is the Father, God is the Son, and God is the Holy Spirit. God, who was the Son, came, and God who is the Holy Spirit is acting now, because all those mechanisms that Jesus had promised have come into play already. Many occurrences are presently taking place, which confirms what was described in the Bible. One of the most notable signs says, "This is how it will be at the end of the age." (Matthew, 13:49). Another referral to the sign of the end of the age is in Matthew, chapter 24. Notice, *not the end of the world, but the end of the age*, meaning *the end of a certain era*. Life will not cease, but all evil will be swept off of the Earth. The waves of Light will do it, which now are growing in pressure.

The second coming of Christ is awaited by many, even though He clearly stated that He wouldn't appear to the world again and that another Advocate will come – the Spirit of Truth, which is another hypostasis of the Creator. "Before long, the world will not see Me anymore" (John, 14:19). "But very truly I tell you, it is for your good that I am going away. Unless I go away, the Advocate will not come to you; but if I go, I will send him to you." (John, 16:7) "And I will ask the Father, and He will give you another advocate to help you and be with you forever – the Spirit of truth." (John, 14:16). Thus, Jesus clearly indicated that *another* hypostasis of the Trinity would come – the Holy Spirit or the Spirit of Truth, which means one will come through *another* Line. Moreover, we were born by this Line. Man is born by the Line of the Holy Spirit; he was created by God's Creative Will. Thus, this Line is sensed, first of all, by our souls.

Our spirit already received the injection of Light a long time ago. And for the past few years, we have been experiencing the increasing pressure *within*. We feel like something is pushing us to explore, and we start searching. It is because our Parent "turned on" this Line, and the intensity of the pressure is rising. It is getting more powerful, invoking our souls to rebel against the lie if we want to survive altogether. And for someone who is not too tightly entwined by the Darkness, who has only small flaws to their character, there is still a chance. Whereas "the goats" no longer have that chance: "When the Son of Man comes in his glory, and all the angels with him, he will sit on his glorious throne. All the nations will be gathered before him, and he will separate the people one from another as a shepherd separates the sheep from the goats. He will put the sheep on his right and the goats on his left." (Matthew, 25:31-33). "Then he will say to those on his left, 'Depart from me, you who are cursed, into the eternal fire prepared for the devil and his angels'…" (Matthew, 25:41). Jesus said about them, "Do not give dogs what is sacred; do not throw your pearls to pigs. If you do, they may trample them under their feet, and turn and tear you to pieces." (Matthew, 7:6). No one will curtsy before them, for the Word serves only good people. When the time comes, there won't be any help for them. However, they are staying for now. I already explained why: they serve as pressure against us in order to drive us under the Law. And they drive many of us, along with our life circumstances. Who creates those circumstances? People do - people who try to snatch every last thing from you. But there is no need to hate them. As strange as it sounds, we need to love them: "Love your enemies" (Matthew, 5:44). Let them live, and they will affect only those who *do not want* to go to God. Then it is well deserved. And the question "Why do people suffer so much?" falls off the table. The answer is *"Because they deserved it, for they do not want to change their ways!"*

By now, it has become quite sickening to live on Earth. We are very tightly closed in by the absolutely impassable clouds of sins. At this time, the Son of Man comes. Moreover, He is "encrypted". If Jesus Christ was allowed to work for over three years, the Second One won't even have three months. Because the evil on Earth is too strong. Thus, the Earth must be prepared for catastrophes, as are happening now. As soon as it nearly reaches the end, as they say, all that remains is to pull the ripcord, then He will be able to openly work for a few weeks, perhaps. At that time, a man will come out, and many of you will see the Cross and the Dove behind him. Just as Christ had the Cross behind and the Dove over Him, there will be one specific person.

The Cross is the symbol of Truth. The Dove is the symbol of the Holy Spirit. The same goes for Christ. Everyone coming from the Trinity has such attributes. And it is impossible for any psychic to forge. Neither for a bunch of psychics nor anyone else. Impossible! It will be a tremendous burst of Light! And He is already somewhere near. That is why Jesus said not to believe anyone! There will be countless liars posing as Prophets. Gospel of Matthew, chapter 24, talks about it. There will be countless false Prophets and false teachers who will be called by His name - Christ. There was already one – Vissarion. He claimed to be Jesus Christ. The last one I know of who proclaimed himself as Christ was Grigory Grabovoy. He announced himself on the Internet as Jesus Christ. The only problem is that they don't know the Bible very well. After all, Jesus said He would not appear on Earth again. But the Other One will come - the Spirit of Truth: "When he comes, he will prove the world to be in the wrong about sin and righteousness and judgment: about sin, because people do not believe in Me; about righteousness, because I am going to the Father, where you can see Me no longer: and about judgment, because the prince of this world now stands condemned. I have much more to say to you, more than you can now bear. But when he, the Spirit of truth, comes, he will guide you into all the truth. He will not speak on his own; he will speak only what he hears, and he will tell you what is yet to come. He will glorify Me because it is from Me that he will receive what he will make known to you. All that belongs to the Father is Mine. That is why I said the Spirit will receive from Me what he will make known to you." (John, 16:7-15). Christ's statements make it evident that He does not speak of His own coming but the coming of another manifestation of God. Jesus is Love, and people crucified Him. And the Spirit of Truth, Immanuel, is the hypostasis of God's Will. *He will descend to establish order on Earth.*

The Spirit of Truth is the Holy Spirit. In the Old Testament (see Isaiah, 7:14), and even in the New Testament, it was mentioned once; He is called Immanuel. "The virgin will conceive and give birth to a son, and they will call him Immanuel" (which means 'God with us')." (Matthew, 1:23). It translates from Hebrew as "God is with us". And who is with us? I am reminding that man is born by the Will of God, the Holy Spirit. That Line of Light, the Holy Spirit, stretched out into the Creation and created the human spirit. Thus, when we make a wrong move, it is immediately registered by that ray of Light, from which we can't hide. This radiation of Light doesn't resemble a ray as we know it. It is all-encompassing, and each person exists within this "light bath". So, each wrong step is recorded: "Wrong, wrong, wrong…" That is the Book of Life. The pages of that Book are our souls, where all of our deeds, good and bad, are recorded. I am explaining this to you in earthly concepts; however, it occurs a little differently. But there is no other way of describing and conveying it to our brain.

So, God is with us through that Line, Immanuel. Immanuel is with us *in spirit*. This is the Line of our Father. Therefore, via this Line comes help, which spreads down to Earth through our souls. That is why we are keenly aware of this help, grace, and support. However, all of this comes under the condition to go and build your Temple. Build it *inside of you*.

It's no use to go and worship somewhere. I am not against going to church. I myself occasionally go to my favorite monastery, the Donskoy, where some very interesting events occur in spirit. It is a very intense place with very powerful radiation of Light. There I received many instructions while I was still weak in spirit. The energy in Moscow is quite heavy, and it was impossible for me to defy. So, I'd go to the Donskoy monastery, where protection is especially strong. There I was given images of what to do, what I *must* do. I was given recommendations when I couldn't see my deficiencies: "You have vanity, pride…" Yes, right! I'd leave there and start fighting my sins again. I was breaking through alone; nobody taught me. But I had that support. So, the Second One, the Son of Man, brings not only the Final Judgment for those who refuse to come under the Law, but also the help, support, and protection for those who have committed to the road of personal rectification.

16. SUFFERING OF A CHILD

Another haunting question for many is "Why do children suffer?" Aren't children innocent creatures?

They are innocent – to a certain point. Let's take a closer look.

A man was born on Earth some time ago, and then he died. His soul left the body because the soul is immortal. Later, the soul came back to Earth again: the man was born, he lived and then died again. So, the soul comes, leaves, and comes back again, and so on. That is how the sequence of reincarnation takes place. First sins were accumulated in the first incarnation. Not understanding the system of redemption of sins through forgiveness, the old sins were brought into the next life, plus the new ones accrued. So, a man came to each life to make a realization and to redeem sins, but he did not! And throughout all these times, the Prophets came, the helpers. They spoke to people, and what did the people do? They either did not listen to the Prophets or listened more intently to the priests than to the essence of religion. Therefore, eventually, we experience the perennial garbage of sins with the new ones added because a man does not change. We can reduce this sinful mass only through humility. Who lives in humility? No one does. Who perceives this world calmly and thanks the Creator for it? No one does. As a result, the accumulation occurs, but there is no unloading. What comes next? Finally, God runs out of patience and says, "Enough!" Man was given many opportunities to change, *but he does not want to!* All nations live this way, generation after generation.

So, when a child is born, he comes and lives in this present life. But his past isn't written off. Because dying as an old man in his previous life, he was a sinner and did not know how to better himself, or maybe he did not want to. Is an elderly man necessarily a holy man? No. Age does not provide holiness. Yes, we must respect the old age and take care of the elderly. However, spiritual matters are quite strict. A man can be left before his death in a state of resentment. He might have accumulated fears and other negativity. Bad words might have been exchanged between the family members and so on. All of it lays like a burden on the human soul, and that load is not redeemed. When will one redeem it? Can we say, "He died, so it's all good, let the evil end"? Not a chance! *What you sow, that must you reap.* We receive only a new body in each reincarnation. But the soul, which is the true heir of our sins, will answer in the present lifetime for all past sins. *The soul that came here again in the body of a newborn carries the burden of all prior responsibilities.* Thus, it is not uncommon that a child starts hurting and suffering, sometimes from day one. That is how it works.

When the soul comes with a load of sins, it gravitates to a certain family according to the Law of Resemblance. It is drawn into the family through resemblance of character. Mom and dad have their own sins, which, when put together, attract a soul that has similar flaws in the character - approximately similar qualities. This is one of the main principles of the inception of the soul or which soul will come to a particular family.

A soul is a guest in the family, and parents take it in. It's not the parents who give birth to the soul, but the Heavenly Father. He gave birth to the eternal spiritual unit. Parents help to incarnate this soul on Earth and to learn and understand life through the Laws of the Creator. The reincarnated soul must try *again* this lesson here. It is inevitable! Until you understand things here on Earth, you cannot leave. The time will pass, and if you have wasted it, you will perish when the entire process of your spiritual education is over. For you did not evolve. Whose fault is that? And who can lead a child out of this sinful quagmire if mom and dad neither understand the point of religion, nor can they provide a truly spiritual upbringing? They themselves are drowning. Naturally, each new generation becomes more sinful, cruder, harsher, more practical, and more rational. That is, intellectuality is growing, and it is obvious. This is the evolution: the frontal lobe of the brain that is responsible for our intellectual abilities is increasing in size. More neurons of the frontal lobe are accruing with each generation. According to the Law of Evolution, only what is in demand develops, leaving the cerebellum, which is responsible for receiving metaphysical information, declining in its ability.

In parapsychology or in esotericism, when this ability of the cerebellum gets restored, they say, "You see, we have given back revelation." Nothing of the sort! *Meditation is not revelation.* Images resulting from meditation come from the Astral World, which is tainted and is controlled by Satan. Satan is influencing the world of our emotions and thoughts. And to break free from his grasp is only possible when you realize your sins and stop sinning while relying on God's Word. Then you will come out of this captivity. And God is your helper. But if you don't want it, or if you lack patience and will, then who is to blame for your weakness? Who is to blame that throughout all those given lives, you did not accumulate either will-power or patience?! These are the *true* human qualities, and intellect has nothing to do with it. Our intellect disintegrates with physical death. And in the next life, a person must be educated again in math, biology, and so on. Then what does the spirit have? What comprises the spiritual strength? *The spiritual strength manifests itself in the ability to overcome obstacles, which requires willpower and patience.*

A man came to Earth. Why did he appear in gross matter at all? It is because the weak spirit needs to become strong. How do we transform from the weak speck of Light into a strong and bright star like the Sun? We came to Earth to overcome obstacles - it's the struggle for life. The more obstacles we overcome, the stronger and more radiant we become as a spirit, so that eventually we may be released from the boundaries of the Physical World. We go through life like a Bootcamp, overcoming one obstacle after another, therefore building our "spiritual muscle" and defeating laziness. Our lightweight spirit was given a polygon in the form of gross matter of the Physical World, which is the only way to conquer indolence. The spirit put on this dense matter of the body, which needs to be fed, clothed, and protected. It is necessary if you want to live! The instinct of self-preservation was created in order for man to value and guard his life. Pain was created to feel the biting of an animal; thus, a man must run and defend himself. It is uncomfortable to be cold and hungry, so he must think, work, progress, which means overcoming obstacles. All of this combines to encourage the development of the spirit. Only one must do it within the limits of the moral Laws. Each time there is a decision to make, you must check in with the Law: "Would I be right acting a certain way?"

However, you found a way to evade this work, submerging into spiritual laziness once again. You deviated from this path and decided to live at someone else's expense, consistently proceeding in moral degradation due to millions of years of deviation from the Law. Thus, you lost the battle for your soul. ***Now arise and try to bring yourselves back to YOU!***

In order to get back on track and to continue on the right path of evolution, one needs, first of all, to obey the Commandments. Then the Law will accept you again and start supporting your upward movement. And if you won't do it, then you will get the opposite – rejection. It's just like when the body rejects the ailing organ. It harms the body, so it must be either operated on or removed. Thus, if a person does not react to preaching and exhortations, he can no longer be "cured". Then there will be an elimination of some part of humanity, like a malignant tumor. And that is what's happening now: more and more people perish under different circumstances, for their time has run out.

That explains why many children are now being born very ill and don't stand a chance in life. It is because they are only young in terms of their bodies; but in spirit, they are just as old as the rest of us.

17. AGE OF THE HUMAN RACE

Once upon a time, we all started this movement together: we descended to Earth and began our spiritual development. Scientists claim that the first human appeared on Earth hundreds of millions of years ago. Unfortunately, our science has gotten very mendacious, especially regarding human origin. There is Darwin's theory, as well as some others. However, it has been proven already that humanity is close to a billion years old. There are some scientific articles on the topic, supporting this theory. Scientist Michael A. Cremo has done some research on the history of the human race. In addition, a piece of monolithic rock dated 2.8 billion years ago was discovered, with the inclusions of metal balls with ring incisions clearly of technical origin. According to spectral analysis, the age of this rock, naturally encasing the balls because they were fused into the rock, is 2.8 billion years. It is 2.8 *billion* years old! If such balls of technological origin were discovered, then the industrial civilization came even earlier than that. When did the anthropoid ape come into being, then? I say, approximately 5.5 billion years ago, where planet Earth is 11 billion years old. Thus, man came to Earth at around the halfway point.

The drilling of extremely deep boreholes found layers estimated to be 200 million years old, which, according to the stratigraphic scale, falls under the Triassic period. Officially, from 250 million years ago began the medieval ages: Mesozoic Era (250-65 million years ago), which includes the Triassic, Jurassic, and Cretaceous periods. So, if the wells are drilled down to 300 million years plus, they either fall in the Triassic, Permian, or Carboniferous periods. There were not even raptors yet, much less a man! And suddenly they find some technology. Upon further exploration, the scientists have found technology dating as far back as nearly billion years. Now we can conclude that the whole scale is wrong. Because according to conventional science, the Precambrian period was over 570 million years ago, which means it was the era that predated the emergence of life on Earth. Officially, the first era of life was Cambrian, then – Ordovician, Silurian, Permian, and so on. And beyond 570 million years was incomprehensibility - Precambrian. And suddenly it turns out, *there was a human*, which was proven by tens and hundreds of findings.

Consequently, our science was mistaken in terms of the age of the human. And why is it so adamantly defending its mistakes? Because Darwin's theory denies God in His relation to us: there is no God, and man descended from the ape by selection and evolution of that ape. We are being told that our relative and our first ancestor is the ape. And God says, "No. You originated from God. You are Light; you are Love! Only you went astray. You are not the apes. You are using the body of the ape as a vessel for your stay on Earth. It was prepared for you. That was planned. If you want to evolve – evolve. But you are not gross matter. Even the ape itself is not the matter, because the soul of the ape came from the Sphere of Animistic Substantiality. But it is not immortal, unlike you are. You are immortal!"

The soul of an animal disintegrates onto composite energies and forms, gathering again later. That is why they have particularly fast modification of species, especially such creators as cockroaches and rats. They immediately accumulate specific information and react to it very fast, so it is not easy to poison the next generation of rats with the same poison. They respond to changes quickly, acquiring new protective properties.

Since we have now touched on the subject of the appearance of the first man on Earth, let's see how it all happened. Take our planetary system. You might know about the work of the Doctor of Technical Sciences, Viktor Plykin. He studied informational properties of water, and I borrowed some of his findings, which coincide with the information given by Abd-Ru-Shin in his book. The results indicate that the Sun was once much cooler. That means its gravitational fields were weaker, as well as the entire field system in general. Once upon a time, there was a very powerful flash on the Sun, causing some mass to separate from it and to begin rotating in the first orbit. That is how planet Earth was born, which is the same way as the other planets. Then the flash happened again, and the mass traveled even farther onto another orbit, then onto the third one, the fourth one, and so on. Finally, the mass cooled down to the point that the first life emerged, such as the blue-green algae that ruled in Earth's waters for millions of years. Then came the time of the mammals, and later of the higher primates, fish, and reptiles. We know this from evolution. Eventually, there came a moment when the human spirit appeared on Earth and embodied the best forms of primates. The primates received this descent of the spirit. Then, those primates who received the spirit began progressing and manifesting into people over the stretch of millions of years, and those who did not receive the spirit remained primates. Darwin could not explain that phenomenon, because it cannot be explained by bare intellect.

Next, there were increasing flashes on the Sun. Of course, those time periods took tens and hundreds of millions of years. In the meantime, the evolution proceeded. And due to what, in fact, were things changing? Who controls the Sun after all? Materialists believe there was an explosion, and the Universe began to expand. They call it the Big Bang. I have read various theories on this topic. I always asked the physicists who wrote those articles and whom I had the opportunity to speak with, "Where did you see an explosion resulting in such ideally coordinated structure of things, where the range of the temperature on Earth is ideal for biomass, and electrons and protons have absolute dependences, constants?" For instance, the weight of a proton is 1836 times greater than that of an electron, always. That is a constant. The charge of negative one is also a constant. There are many other constants, such as light, gravitation, and so on. However, the constants of gravitation, as well as some others, can change due to gravity. The higher the intensity of the gravitational field, the farther away the Sun can hold the planet, i.e., at another distance; this is because gravity is changing.

It has been proven by scientists that the gravitational field influences the concept of time: the higher the intensity of the gravitational field, the faster the processes occur inside that field. When the process accelerates, then time changes. The simplest definition of time is the speed of life, which is the speed of development of certain processes. There is nothing complicated about this concept. So, processes take place inside of some space, and they develop at a specific rate; this is time. It registers changes, such as it was small and became big, or it was foolish and became wise, perhaps 20 years later. Or maybe it was stupid and became even more stupid over 40 years. The process goes on. Everyone does according to their will: either develops or eventually degrades.

Right now, we are positioned at a certain distance from the Sun - about 150 million kilometers. That distance from Earth to the Sun is called the astronomical unit. Let's call the present radius of the distance from the Sun $R2$. Suppose the first people on Earth appeared when the radius $R1$ was 15 million kilometers, roughly speaking. So, now $R2 = 10R1$. Let's apply the formula $2\pi R$ = circumference of the orbit, where R is variable, and 2π is a constant value. That means the circumference of the orbit changes with radius.

When the first man came and inhabited Earth, the spiritual development began. Do you remember the biblical centenarians? They were 800-900 years old. Back then, years were also counted by the number of revolutions around the Sun. If $2\pi R$ was ten times smaller, respectively, there were ten times more years. That means 80-90 life-years *now* equal to 800-900 revolutions around the Sun *back then*. Thus, there was nothing miraculous, and there were no centenarians. The Bible precisely coincides with this knowledge.

Why were these changes taking place on our planet? It is because time on Earth throughout its entire existence has not always been uniform. Gravity was not uniform; the constants were changing. Time was homogenous only during the last loop of 60-70 thousand years. The speed of life was constant *only* in this period. But prior to that, it was slower for a certain number of years. And before that, it was even slower than that. So, going further back into the centuries, time was slower and slower. The reason is that the first man on Earth cannot be given a very fast pace of life. Imagine that some being entered a foreign world and into the body of a primate. It needed time to understand this life, so the processes were happening very slowly.

After tens of millions of years had passed, the first selection took place. The ones that were wrong in their development were weeded out. The rest entered into the new regimen of time. This event took place many times throughout the history of humanity. So, all these rounds were different civilizations. There were over 200 civilizations and not 5 or 6, as the esoteric says. Not at all. Humanity has been given *many chances* to evolve, but we still are not evolving! Even the laziest spirit was given all the time in the world, but it did not want to evolve.

Thus, now it is as if God is telling us, "I have made everything possible for you! The time was given, perhaps five times longer than the laziest person would need. I sent you the helpers throughout history. They came, and came, and came at all times and to many nations. The last ones, as you remember, were Krishna, who came 5000 years ago, Zoroaster – 3000 plus years ago, Moses – 3000 years ago, Jesus – 2000 years ago. What else do you need?! What do you want from Me?! When I came here Myself in the person of Christ, you killed Him! How else can I speak with you? How else can I help you? You are hopeless!"

Therefore, the new tactic comes into play. The last one is coming, the one called the Son of Man in the Bible, and with His coming, the Final Judgment will happen. The Bible says it in Christ's words. The coming of the Son of Man *is* the Final Judgment (refer to the Gospel of Matthew, 25:31-46). The Son of Man will take those who want to go to God and will help them, and the rest will be eliminated — eliminated not by God, but *by their own evil*. God will remove His protection, and then people will be left one on one with the evil they have created.

The evil that *you* bring to the world will be returned to you through the worst kind of people. You will be either crushed or will come under the shield of the Law. But the Law will only protect those who obey It. And that is fair. There is no other way. Once again, that is the function of the Law: to punish people for their sins and to protect those who overcome them.

18. E=MC²

Now, let's talk briefly about physics of space and physics of the soul. Returning to Illustration 1: there is Infinity that radiates energy, and there is the Creation, where we reside. This Creation is a series of waves that form many layers. And what are the borders of these layers? We all know of the point light source. Have you ever happened to be on the outskirts where there is just one lamp on the pole? Looking at the lamp, you can see the first circle of light very clearly, and the second one is barely noticeable. This optical phenomenon is called a halo. Usually, you can observe it in rural areas where there are no other light interferences. In the city, we have too much light coming from different directions. You can see that these glowing circles are concentric. There are many circles spreading farther from the light, but they fall out of our angstrom, our eyes cannot catch them. That is the infrared radiation and similar.

Our Creation was made according to the same principle, and all these borders are characteristic lines. Only naturally, the scale is enormous. So, within two borders, space and time bear specific characteristics. How is the hierarchy formed? Below the Spiritual World is the Sphere of Animistic Substantiality, then the Ethereal World and, finally, physical or manifested matter. I am reminding you of the famous formula: $E = MC^2$. The word "energy" is translated from Greek as "activity". So, energy means activity. Thus, some activity, in this case emanating from God, eventually manifests into a mass if we subtract speed C, meaning if we slow down this energy E. We can say that matter is frozen energy, and the formula $E=MC^2$ is the formula of the creation of the world. This formula is quite brilliant. We read it as energy equals mass accelerated to the squared speed of light. If we speed up the mass of matter to 90 billion kilometers per second (C^2), what will we get? If we accelerate matter to such a speed, it will turn into energy - a different state. That is a simple, well known scientific postulate.

So, we have the energy that flows from the Creator at a colossal speed. If we gradually remove some speed from it, zero by zero, it will eventually come to the state of the speed of light, and then some matter will begin to form into different shapes made of electrons and protons. All of this happens mostly during the transition from the Ethereal to the Physical World. If we approach from the opposite direction, i.e., from the World of Physical Matter and up, we will see that on the border of the Physical and Astral worlds starts the phenomenon of the first acceleration of speed. The scientists studying this field create accelerators – cyclotrons. They accelerate particles and get completely different properties of those particles. The faster a particle is accelerated, the more its properties change. Eventually, those particles start to divide into smaller ones. If we investigate in greater depth, we will see that the entire border will eventually taper off into a "triangle" of various speeds. The closer to God, to the Source, the greater the energy, meaning the speeds are colossal. The dynamic is increasing; thus, the particles are becoming ever smaller. And then the world of this matter ends, and a completely foreign world begins at the level of the Ethereal World. The Ethereal World is built based on the same Laws, but it has different constants due to the speed. The main limitation of the Physical World is the speed of light, which means that physical matter does not have a greater speed. Even the borderline between the Physical and Ethereal worlds has a speed 400 times greater. It is a transitional border between the physical and ethereal matters, and it is very small. This transition is the border state of matter. Further, the Ethereal World might have an additional 20-30 zeroes. I did not investigate it using specific numbers. If you get to the higher level of the Animistic Substantiality, i.e., closer to God, it is even faster - add another 100 zeroes or so, and the Spiritual World is even faster than that. So, life closer to God is faster and more dynamic.

The human spirit is born in faster life - in the Spiritual World. Naturally, we all like fast driving or riding; well, those who have no fear. In general, people like speed. When we have dreams of flying, we really enjoy it. That is because we *want* this speed! We have a completely different speed of life in spirit. In spirit we change much faster than in the body. Thus, in spirit we are very fast, whereas in the body, we are slow, and our development is slow, and we know it. I changed in spirit fairly quickly and received my first dividends within a few months, but my body succumbed to these changes much slower. Major diseases left my body. Although, occasionally, I still had minor health problems. But eventually, little by little, my body was completely repaired.

In the Physical World, time flows at a specific pace. The greater the speed of the wave of energy, the faster time passes, because the wave sets the rhythm of time. I will explain why this happens. What is a wave, after all? It is the sequence of peaks of fluctuations. One fluctuation per second is called one Hertz. Meaning, it is the peak strike of the wave at some object. You can compare it to hitting a nail with the hammer – one strike means one wave has passed. So, if we hit 2, 3, 4 times, we will have 2, 3, 4 waves. The more Hertz per second, the higher the density of the fluctuations. Consequently, each peak is one strike at an object.

When I started changing spiritually, I was slow at first, but I was getting faster and faster with each passing month. When I treated a patient, the healing sessions would last 2-3 hours at first. I had patients with asthma, tumors, and other illnesses. Later, I became faster, and now the sessions are very short. Why did this happen? Because the density of the waves increased. That is the frequency of the fluctuations. Frequency of the fluctuations, if anybody knows a little physics, is the spectrum. So, the spectrum was changing from infrared to red, to orange, to yellow, and so on towards the ultraviolet. After that begins the x-ray (roentgen) radiation, according to the wavelength. The x-ray is the penetration into the structure, meaning I can see through a physical body. That is the secret of extrasensory healers - the radiation changes. It is when the wavelength operates and fits into the visible objects. The human eye is just like any other wave. When I look at a visible object, and one wave fits into it, I can see that object. If my wavelength is longer, I cannot see it; it is too small for me. When your radiation is changing, your wavelength is decreasing, and the density of the wave is increasing. Thus, the electromagnetic spectrum is shifting towards the higher parameter in frequency and energy.

Moreover, if you are climbing your spiritual stairs higher and higher in the process of evolution, you are transitioning to the other wave speeds as you conquer many steps of the Astral World. And then, when you are passing beyond the Astral World, you can see *clearly* the lie of this world. That is the essence of the core exhortation of Christ – *no one will get there other than through Him!* And Jesus was the Word. Eat this Word, drink It, meaning ***make the Commandments your way of life***. If you really do it – conquer all of your vices on all levels, including the emotional level, then you come out beyond the boundaries of the Astral World. All the lies are confined only into the Physical and Astral worlds. Beyond that is your soul. You are connected with your soul, and your soul is connected with God. Then the radiation that you will start conducting into your body won't let you be deceived by any false ideas anymore. For your sensitivity will be too high. A lie won't even be able to get near you. Charged with the Light, you will become too strong for that. Naturally, your radiation will be changing. Here on Earth, we measure radiation by waves. The wave density is the fluctuation frequency or the amplitude. The wavelength is inversely proportional to the fluctuation period $L = 1/T$, and it is always changing in the process of spiritual evolution. *The purer your soul becomes, the more abilities you are given.*

19. FREEDOM FROM SIN

As a result of personal experience, the tough experience of conquering your sins, you will eventually receive the dividends in the form of physical health and good fortune, just like I did. And I want to share this knowledge. When you accomplish it, you get overfilled with strength, this abundant energy (E). It comes, and you have to give it away. But until you have accumulated your own, until you have pulled that log out of your own eye, how can you share an experience that you yourself do not have? "Why do you look at the speck of sawdust in your brother's eye and pay no attention to the plank in your own eye? How can you say to your brother, 'Let me take the speck out of your eye', when all the time there is a plank in your own eye? You hypocrite, first take the plank out of your own eye, and then you will see clearly to remove the speck from your brother's eye." (Matthew, 7:3-5). First, you must have the experience of pulling the log out of your eye - your own snags. When I mastered it, I saw that it led me to good health and other fortunes. Then I concluded that this design really works! It turns out that religion is alive! I discovered that Christianity gives great results if you take the words of Jesus and *start living by them* instead of quoting biblical phrases all day long as they do in the churches. What's the use in that?

So, when you make the Commandments your way of life and see real benefits from it, you, first of all, prove it to yourself, which grants you a great blessing. Then you start handing it to others. Throughout the years, many people have gathered and began showing results. I am speaking of those who are working and not letting themselves be deceived. Others are letting themselves be tricked into some conflicting ideas, which means the training does not ensure the person's breakthrough. The training is like any other school where you are taught a subject and given all the necessary tools, but you are the one who has to use them. If you are not putting your knowledge to practice, you won't be a very good professional, which is especially noticeable in spirit. For example, it is when a person is stuck on a lower level of spiritual evolution, all the while thinking very highly of himself, creating a lot of noise around his persona because vanity hasn't been conquered. Vanity is like rose-colored glasses and an absolute absence of self-criticism. Some people ask me, "What is there in me that is so bad? I'm not doing anything awful." And I ask them, "Are you a saint?" "No." "So, you have something to work on?" "Yes, I do." "Then keep working." "On what?" "Why don't you want to look for it yourself? Are you in trouble? Are you dying?" "No, everything is ok." "Then get yourself together and start looking." "Can't you give me a hint?" "I can give you a hint once, but if I always do so, you won't make any effort. There is no struggle." Struggling means forcing yourself to work - forcing your spirit to work, as well as your brain. If everything is handed to you, like I am giving to you based on my experience, then you won't accumulate *your own* experience! You won't be participating in the process. But everyone equally will have to take the test on spiritual maturity and receive a certificate, figuratively speaking. Then, when the Judgment begins, you won't be answering to me but to the Creator. It will apply *to you!* What have *you* done if you've always been begging and expecting a handout instead of searching yourself? But most people would much rather have a handout because they are lazy.

That is why I can always sense very keenly with my soul when I don't want to help a person. Maybe I helped multiple times in the past with pleasure, but suddenly I get the feeling that I don't want to help anymore. Then I ask myself, "Why?" And my soul, which is linked to God, tells me, "Enough helping the lazy one. You are corrupting him!" I am receiving refusal at the level of my intuitive perception: "I don't want to help." If I ignore that signal and start helping, I will start experiencing misfortunes in my life. It's a vicious cycle: I am wrong, and I will get spanked. If I am helping the person in this particular case, I am corrupting him. Corrupting means you are not doing any good. You are doing harm, thinking that you are doing good. I was taught that way pretty strictly. Because conquering your own sins and teaching others how to do it are two different things.

While you are battling with your own demons, your intentions are different, which brings on a different dynamic. Let's say I needed to get rid of some negative character traits. I had fears, vanity, resentment, irritability, anger, which is the highest phase of irritability. I also had jealousy and maybe some other little flaws. I had to destroy them each time they appeared. All these emotions create otherworldly forms. And those are thousands and thousands of forms! Take an emotion like fear. How many times in my life have I gotten scared? Perhaps, in my past life as well. Our ancestors called those forms "demons": "a demon of fear, a demon of jealousy, a demon of anger took over you…" I've created those demons and counted them already – hundreds of thousands! And each one of them requires redemption. I was walking the walk, redeeming them with humility, and not creating any more. I was enduring and working. Thus, I started accumulating will, and my patience has grown. Those qualities were the products of my work. What happened next? *My spirit began to free itself from sins.* Each year I had less of these negative character traits. **Elimination of negativity from one's own character is the concept of freedom.** A human is a spirit. Thus, my spirit became free.

Jesus once said this phrase: "Everyone who sins is a slave to sin." (John, 8:34). Why? Because one cannot resist it! He still feels afraid, irritated, jealous, and so on. You are slaves to these negative qualities of your character. You have accumulated them for thousands of years, from generation to generation. And now your personal will isn't enough to conquer them. But the Higher Will comes through the Line of the Father and gives your spirit the injection of will. However, for that to happen, you must desire it *yourself,* sincerely, and with all your heart and soul! You have to believe first and then start walking this road. *Only then* will you be given this subsidy. And if you are not doing it, if your faith is weak or you don't want to fight for yourself, then the help won't come. This notion falls under the Law of Freedom of Choice.

Man, in his laziness, delves so deep into money-making and growing his potatoes and cucumbers that he forgets where he came from. He forgets that he was born Up Above. *We have forgotten our origin and now are seriously punished for this forgetfulness.* So, the Wise God is looking at us from Above as if thinking, "Do you really lack the courage to rise from your knees and fight back this whole wickedness, which simply seized you in the net? Fight back! You have the strength *and a helper.* Only you must work cooperatively. There is help only when you yourselves are going. No going – no help; that is the Law of Freedom of Choice." God is bound by His Law and cannot help you until *you yourself* start coming to Him. His Law is holy to Him, and He, unlike men, does not break It. If you don't take a few steps toward God, He cannot help you! *He is bound by the Law. You do not choose Him; thus, He cannot help you.* That is the Law! *You* must take the first step!

Taking the first step doesn't mean to drop on the ground, screaming "God, help me! I accept You! I believe in You!" God says, "This isn't moving towards Me. That is what your sinful churches taught you. The moving to Me is, in fact, *moving* and not stomping and chattering. You in your words are going to Me and believing in Me, but you refuse to work on yourself." You made a mess on this Earth, and do you think that God will come and clean everything up for you and redeem everything with His blood, just like the churches taught you? Not a chance! That is a terrible sin that the churches have committed, deceiving you and a great many other people. *God acts differently*. If you start correcting yourself, God is your helper. If not, God won't help you. You must make the first move, *for God does not need you, but you need God*. Understand this superposition at last! No one will babysit you, trying to convince you of anything. If you want to look for God, do it! If you don't believe, it is your choice. No one is forcing you to believe or is pressing you to go to God. No. Your life is your judgment. And if this judgment is pushing your limits to the point that your life becomes unbearable, perhaps *only then* you'll be compelled to change. If you don't want to do it voluntarily, then wait until the life circumstances drive you to where you can't stand it anymore. It happened to me many years ago. Some people approach me now, saying that their lives are sickening. Wouldn't that be great if a man woke up one day, got out of bed, and said, "God, I'm coming! I've realized everything!" There are no such people — almost none, anyway. Maybe they exist, but I haven't met them. Most people come to it due to their troubles. And to create those troubles, some unpleasant people are needed. I repeat, *God is tolerating bad people on Earth for now and letting them stay because they are needed.* They also serve God. They are the herders. They herd us under the Law. You need to understand this concept. And man doesn't realize it, demanding, "God, our Holy Father, help me! I am not doing so well!" He is expecting God to rush to him: "Oh, where are you, my beloved? I'll amend everything for you at once." And how does the amendment happen? Again, not according to the Church.

What does the Church teach us? That God is all-forgiving. He loves us and will always forgive, as long as you live right. But because man doesn't live right and God is all-forgiving, he hopes, in the worst-case scenario, to go to a church where in God's name they'll forgive all of his sins. Only sins aren't forgiven that way! So, the vicious cycle continues. Eventually, some very stubborn believer might cry out, "God, help me! Forgive me!" and God does send forgiveness… in the form of punishment, **because there is no other form of forgiveness**. A person gets some negative occurrence in life, but he doesn't embrace it: "God, I asked You for help, but instead, I am in trouble again." God says, "If I could converse with you, I would tell you that I forgive you through this trouble, only you must accept it in humility." The punishment *is* forgiveness, but you do not accept it with humility. Moreover, your rejection is *doubling* your sin. So, instead of being forgiven, your sin is *restored* because you did not redeem it, and your incorrect attitude is doubling it. The next phase is the consequences of the same sin will come into your life again, except then they will be *intensified.* If you don't embrace it then, it will come back *even greater* (see Illustration 3, the bag of Karma). This pattern continues, creating the scenario you see now. This wave is growing and coming towards us like a tsunami of our sins. Not knowing how to accept it with humility, we will eventually be crushed by this tsunami. That is the system, and we didn't invent it. We are guests in this Creation. And the Host is the one establishing Laws here.

So, by the Law of Choice, man must take the first step. And what is the first step? You might say, "God, I'm coming to you!" but in reality, you don't even have faith. Open yourself up and try having faith; start battling your vices. At least start! *Then* you will receive help. That is how it works! But man is waiting for proof of God's existence: "Show me first! First, help me, and then I'll decide whether I want to take it on." Wrong approach! This is also very important to understand.

The freedom of spirit is, in fact, the freedom from your sins. You then become free to act as your soul desires. When I felt this freedom, I realized that there are no such Laws that my spirit is *forced* to obey against its will, just like the book *In the Light of Truth* says. There are only my spiritual abilities, which were locked from me by my sins. How can these fast waves, this treasure, be given to someone who still continues to be offended? If I would get offended at my wife or my daughter, using such fast waves, I would simply kill them! I understood that those waves were locked from me. Even the psychics who have only unlocked a small border of the Astral World, 400C, already do so much harm. There are home-grown psychics, and there are professionals who work in Intelligence. Luckily, those people are directed at our enemies. What if they were directed at us? You can kill a person, stop his heart if you are good at concentrating such high-speed waves. That type of equipment already exists. Tremendous harm can be done using the wave of just 400C. Who can those psychics affect? Only the ones who are lower in type – either materialists or those underdeveloped in faith. But a person who came to a state of fighting their demons and started going the route of spiritual evolution while growing in faith eventually becomes invincible.

Jesus Christ came (just like the Second Messenger came now) and gave us the corridor towards the exit from the captivity of our demons. This corridor is the breakthrough from our sins gathered at the level of the Astral World. Jesus said, "I am the way and the truth and the life. No one comes to the Father except through Me." (John 14:6). *To enter this corridor, you must obey His Word.*

20. BUILDING YOUR TEMPLE

Abd-Ru-Shin writes in his book that, ultimately, the human spirit has no Laws. Meaning, if man regains his spiritual component, he will no longer view the Laws of his Creator as something he is *obligated* to obey; *it will be his <u>natural desire</u>.* The human spirit *automatically* follows the Laws of God.

For instance, take an ordinary man, like any of you. You don't want to kill anybody, or rob someone, be rude, say an obscene word, or do other nasty things that average people lack in their nature. Is somebody forcing you to be this way? No. *It is human nature.* Human nature: we are born from God, and all good qualities are embedded in us. Those qualities are the natural, typical character traits. Then why are we behaving erroneously? Due to our laziness, ignorance, vanity, or pride. One starts to desire more than he earned: "Everyone does it, why can't I?" That is how debauchery and corruption begin. If your soul succumbs to it, it takes that route. And the soul that doesn't succumb to it suffers and wonders, "I am an honest and a decent person. I live by my labor. Why am I suffering?" I already answered this question. If you allow a little bit of delinquency, God cannot help you. One must start reducing his delinquency. As long as we are reducing it, a dynamic occurs, so help keeps coming. If we are not reducing it, there is no help. And to reduce it, we need our will and patience. We don't even need much intellect. Intellect is needed for teaching this concept: to explain in the simplest logical words what is happening. But to battle yourself on the inside, silently, no great intellect is needed. You only need to understand this system, and then what? *All that is required are will and patience. We must cultivate these qualities within us.*

The Bible instructs that your Temple is built on the inside: "Do you not know that you yourselves are God's temple and that God's Spirit dwells in your midst?" (1 Corinthians, 3:16). "The coming of the Kingdom of God is not something that can be observed, or will people say, 'Here it is', or 'There it is', because the Kingdom of God is in your midst." (Luke, 17:20). The Temple is *within* us, just like the Bible says, and we must start looking inward, paying attention to our *inner world*. The Temple is not made of bricks; it is created with our spiritual qualities. When the Temple gets built, your spirit comes and now inhabits it. But we must build it first!

The first rock, the foundation of our Temple, is comprised of _faith_ and _repentance_ (Illustration 9). Let's discuss faith first. Jesus once said, "Blessed are the poor in spirit, for theirs is the Kingdom of Heaven." (Matthew, 5:3). This quote was incorrectly translated, and the word "begging" was replaced by the word "poor". Poor in spirit means _weak in spirit._ But it is also written that the Kingdom of Heaven is taken by strength - the strength of the spirit: "From the days of John the Baptist until now, the Kingdom of Heaven was subjected to violence, and violent people have been raiding it." (Matthew, 11:12). In this context, violence means spiritual strength. What comprises spiritual strength? Will, patience, and strong faith. Strong faith is when your spirit is still alive and not withered away like a plant in a desert. It can fight off its own demons and break through. That's what the strong spirit is. And how can the "poor in spirit" break through to anywhere? It's like expecting a person whose legs are paralyzed to get up and walk! So, in His Sermon on the Mount, Jesus referred to the ones _begging_ in spirit, i.e., those who are _pleading with their spirit, for this is the only way to be heard by God._ Begging God isn't done with the "microchip" of your brain. Those are the waves of 300,000 km/sec. And not even with your feelings; those waves are 400 times greater, which is the field of the theurgists, who are the liars, false prophets, and false teachers who drew people under their banners. Anyone who is not practicing religion _through the Commandments_ will not get to that Kingdom. _That person is deceived!_ Thus, faith has to be spiritual. We have spirit; so, faith must be born in spirit. Faith is the state of your soul. Real faith is not a result of you thinking about whether you do or don't believe in God. _Thinking_ about faith doesn't amount to faith. Even the _feeling_ is not faith. But your _intuitive perception_ is faith. True faith comes from the realm of intuitive perceptions. Feeling and intuitive perception are two different radiations. Intuitive perception is neither a feeling nor a thought. People cannot distinguish between them, but they have to.

Thinking supports our logic on Earth; it is an assessment of the world of manifested matter. Our feelings, we can't clearly explain even them, must be separated from intuitive perceptions. We must learn how to do it. Feelings, after all, also support us in this world. But in the Higher World, we cannot exist without our intuitive perceptions. They serve us there as a gauge. If this gauge is "silent", then we are blind, we cannot navigate in that World. It's like being blind, deaf, and mute in this world. How will one get by in this World then? He is crippled.

LOVE

THE TRUTH

KNOWLEDGE

TEMPLE OF THE SOUL

WILL   PATIENCE

HUMILITY
CONTROL OVER THOUGHTS
GOAL
FAITH AND REPENTANCE

III.9

Thus, ultimately, we are *spiritually crippled* until we restore our upper spiritual hypostasis. It is our "I". It is our *core*. How can we live without it? We have forgotten about this quality, settled in our tiny little world, and consider ourselves great, knowledgeable, and wise. We call ourselves "homo sapiens", which is Latin for "wise man". What kind of sapiens are we if we poisoned our own lives?! We are destroying this world, each one of us with our own behavior. And many consider themselves innocent, pointing fingers: "Those are the bad ones, they did it!" Then I say, "What about our past? We lived there and also created some sins." (Illustration 3). In sum, each one of us made our own contribution to world destruction. There are no sinless people. *Each one of us is only answering for our personal sins*, and now the pressure of retribution is rising. "There is a time for everything... a time to scatter stones and a time to gather them..." (Ecclesiastes, 3:5). I say to you: *that time to gather has come!*

So, our brain generates thoughts. Concentrated thoughts are what is referred to as "hypnosis". Our astral cloak generates feelings, and the concentration of these feelings is called "occultism" or meditation. But our intuitive perceptions are generated by our spirit, and concentrated intuitive perceptions lead to *revelation* and not to meditation. Such ability is earned *only* by obeying the Commandments. The Bible talks about the experiences in spirit, or revelations, when an angel appears and shows what will be. "One of the seven angels who had the seven bowls came and said to me..." "Then the angel carried me away in the Spirit into a wilderness." (Revelation 17:1, 17:3).

True faith is the state of your soul. When I believe, it's like my boundaries are ending, and I am merging with something infinite. When true faith comes to you, this is how you feel.

With faith comes *repentance*, because you realize your mistakes and wrongdoings before men and before God. Then you repent from the bottom of your heart and ask for forgiveness. For that, you don't even have to go to church or to confess to a priest. One can do it without leaving their home. If you are genuine in your repentance, it will be registered Up Above, and some relief will come, for as we know "Penitent heads don't get chopped off" (proverb).

The second rock is a *goal*. The main goal for man is to free his soul. It must prevail over any earthly goals. The Darkness will always try to derail you by throwing earthly problems at you to solve, keeping your attention away from the primary goal. ***Without making your soul a priority, you will never win this battle.*** "No one can serve two masters. Either you will hate the one and love the other, or you will be devoted to the one and despise the other. You cannot serve both God and money." (Matthew, 6:24). "Therefore, I tell you, do not worry about your life, what you will eat or drink, or about your body, what you will wear." (Matthew, 6:25). "But seek first His Kingdom and His righteousness, and all these things will be given to you as well." (Matthew, 6:33). Keep that in mind.

The next stone is *control over thoughts*. The brain is our instrument of logic. Our intellect demands us to connect all the dots and explain to ourselves the point of religion. Our brain wants to be convinced of the necessity of exploring the relationship between man and God. When I first attempted to think "vertically", I noticed that my brain refused to serve me. I simply could not form a single logical thought. It was as if someone turned a fan on in my head, and all my thoughts started moving chaotically. When I had to solve any earthly problems pertaining to work or family, my brain worked just fine. As soon as I switched to the topic of "me and God", immediately interferences would appear in the form of various undesirable thoughts. It was as if my brain no longer belonged to me. I could not think straight.

After nearly a month of struggling with it, I concluded that my brain doesn't solely belong to me, and I am not the master of my own brain. Literally so! I was astonished by this discovery! That means there is some *invisible force* that imposes specific thoughts on me disguised as my own. But in order for me to continue with my spiritual investigation, I knew I had to find a way to submit my brain to my will. Somehow, I had to regain full control over my thoughts if I wanted to learn anything about my relationship with God. And I came up with a solution.

In the past, I used to read a lot of science fiction books, and I remembered a story that gave me an idea. Eventually, I invented a method that I called "concentrating". I took a plain pencil and thought about the technological process of manufacturing it. That is, I played the entire manufacturing process step by step in my head, picturing it in images. This exercise only takes me a minute or two, but while I am doing it, the Darkness is unable to interfere with my thinking. It cannot interrupt my train of thought; it cannot "squeeze in". After some time, the Darkness gave up on me, and I started regaining control over my thoughts. When I got rid of that undesirable influence, I could finally see what my problems were and how to solve them. This technique took me a while to master. But eventually, I was able to think clearly and, therefore, see a *simple logic* behind religion. *That logic explained to my brain why I needed God in my life.*

To this day, I occasionally use the method of concentrating when I feel the Darkness trying to take over my head, or when I feel that my mind is clouded or fixated on a thought that is hard to get rid of. This occurs when you don't want to think of something, but the thought keeps playing in your head like a broken record, becoming a real nuisance. When this happens, the concentrating works well. It is a weapon against demons trying to feed you certain thoughts that undermine your personal spiritual work.

When you apply this method, you can picture any process, whether it is cooking a dish for dinner, making your way to work, or manufacturing a pencil. The main point is to continuously picture one step after another fast enough to ensure there are no gaps between the images so that the dark forces are unable to infiltrate those gaps. We used to believe that all thoughts born in our head are ours, but it isn't so. *Unfortunately, nobody looked for Satan under cover of "rational mind" or intellect. Surprisingly, that is exactly where he resides, introducing thoughts that lead us to destruction if we accept them.*

The next stone of our Temple is *humility*. It is an *essential* stone because, without humility, there is no redemption of sins. Humility is an ultimate weapon against demons. **Humility kills a demon!** I forgive, and God's Will eliminates that demon. If I forgave 100 times, 100 demons were destroyed. That is the *real* death of the Darkness. Thus, it enters a very serious battle with us. But the Will of God gives us protection. It doesn't let us drown, which I have experienced. I was told, "You can't fight the Darkness. It has been reinforced for centuries, thousands, millions of years! We keep generating it, adding to the enormous mass. What man can conquer it?" I say, a man cannot, but the Will of God can. If I am honest before God's Will, meaning I am trying to bring myself to It through my best behavior, It begins to protect me. Then I can win this battle and move forward. That is the rule. We must know the rules.

This concept of real humility isn't taught by the Church. Various Christian churches have been leading us for 2000 years now, and nothing good emerged from it, with the exception of a few single cases - people who broke away from under the Church's dogma. Do you remember the story of Sergius of Radonezh? He left society and went into the woods, away from the Church. He beat his demons in the wilderness where he lived 30 kilometers away from the nearest settlement. He fought his sins for 20-30 years and began conquering them *outside of the Church's dogma*. He realized that self-righteously walking in front of the pulpit with the incense censer wouldn't bring him any closer to God; to achieve that, he had to conquer his sins. Indeed, there is no sense in such church rituals. To speak and not do is hypocrisy.

So, the four stones (faith and repentance, goal, control over your thoughts, and humility) are the basis, the foundation of any religion. And an individual has to build on these qualities.

Next, the walls of the Temple are built of two qualities – *patience* and *will*. If your will is not supported by your patience, it will last you only for a "cavalry charge" against your sins. And you have to fight them long and consistently, accumulating *experience* and *knowledge*. The experience produces knowledge. The concept of knowledge must be strictly regarded, just like any other concept. Knowledge is not what a person once read in the Bible and now can say, "I know, I read the Bible." I say, "But you have never grasped its spiritual meaning; thus, you don't know the essence of the Bible." They counter with, "Yes, I do know it, and I can quote it from any page!" I respond, "So what? A parrot also can say many words, but he doesn't understand what he is saying." A particular stand-up comedian used to say, "Scientists are the people who know a lot, but the wise are the ones who actually *understand* what they know." That is a big difference.

Thus, our will, supported by our patience, eventually creates the rise of the Temple. The walls are rising. Finally, the dome is born – *the knowledge*, as a result of many years of experience. And, in the end, you begin to understand the essence of *Love*, which is the Cross! The symbol of Truth! Then your Temple is completed.

21. HEAVENLY LOVE

We don't understand what Love is. The phrase "Love your enemy" either seems incredibly stupid or, at least, makes us feel completely ignorant. Why do I have to love or bless my enemy? I have already explained why we need to love our enemies. Heavenly Love, which comes from the Creator (God is Love), is the *strictness and justice* of the Law. If I am bullied by an enemy, I will respond. If he tries to take my territory or destroy my family, I will resist him. I have that right by the Law of God's Love. Only I must do it with no anger towards him. *I must defend myself without breaking the Law of God* - this is the art of living, and we must learn to apply it.

Strictness and justice of Heavenly Love apply to parental love as well. If you want to raise a strong individual, a decent person capable of understanding all aspects of life, both intellectual and spiritual, you will do it as a parent! If your child starts to shirk, becomes lazy, you will apply more pressure, forcing him to act right. But if you neglect him, the child grows up unruly and begins to harm society with his negative character traits. Only, in the end, he is harming himself. What kind of parental love is this? It is *anti-love* if you aren't raising him right. As a parent, you must be very clear in explaining the system of religion when the time comes and say, "If you want to be a respectable, healthy, strong individual, capable of experiencing true love in life, you must learn to love *first. Only then* love will come to you. If you don't know how to love, you will never be given true love in life." That is the Law of this world - *give* and only then will you be rewarded! What can you give except your crooked personality? If things don't go your way, there comes irritability, grievance, and jealousy.

And what is jealousy? Many equate this emotion with an expression of love. However, it has nothing to do with love. Jealousy is when one assumes a position - if I love someone, then that person is mine. That is *sensual* love. But *true love* comes from a realm of intuitive perceptions. Faith, hope, and love are intuitive perceptions, not feelings. Love from the intuitive perception emanates from your soul. *That kind of love never demands anything.* It doesn't demand a woman I love to belong to me, to look only at me, to think only about me, and to do what I want. No! Love is complete freedom for that woman. Love is when you say, "I love you very much, but I want you to be happy with or without me. If you don't like me, be happy with someone else." If a woman I love chooses to leave, I will be very sad without her, but I feel the greatest tact and respect towards her and won't bother her if she doesn't like me. That is love! Who is capable of such love? Those cases are very rare, perhaps existing only in legends and myths. You may see it once in a while, but it is short-lived, and later, it all crumbles. Why? Because a couple *cannot* oppose the onslaught of the evil of this world. This world is oriented on profit and sensual pleasures because we are ruled by our vices.

As soon as real love begins to sprout between a man and a woman, all evil like a pack is thrown in to destroy it, and the battle begins. Why does it happen? Jesus was Love. Thus, Antichrist is Anti-Love. ***In Love lies liberation for the soul.*** If people would love each other with their soul, and not just their own woman, child, or man, but people as people, always wishing them well – they would be benevolent and in a state of all-time help and support. ***When people learn to live in love for one another, it will be the kind of Love Jesus commanded.*** That kind of Love alone destroys the Darkness. Because such Love encompasses all the goodness in people and brings out those qualities which then start overcoming the negative character traits that a person might possess. Love is *the strongest* weapon against demons; therefore, the Darkness won't rest until it either destroys love or is destroyed by love.

On Earth, Heavenly Love also encompasses the concept of sensuality and physical attraction. It is a tribute to nature. Unfortunately, we have taken it too far. It is not so essential to us. The full harmony is when the Light descends and enters the body only due to Eros. The concept of Eros has a much broader sense than people usually associate it with. Eros is a conduit of Heavenly Love into the body. That Heavenly Love nourishes our spirit.

Refer to Illustration 10. God is Love. He also gave birth to Will and Love – the human spirit. For the spirit to enter the body, it needs to be transformed. Once again, the spirit is a very fast being. The waves are colossal in terms of speed. They need to be slowed down. And our cloaks serve as a cascade of wave converters. They transform and transfer the high-speed waves into the slow ones. Our body is rather the slow world – the physical matter, and it can only absorb these slow waves. The waves cool down as they distance from the Source. When the slowdown happens, at some point, the waves begin to separate. They cannot stay together because there is no adhesion.

CREATOR

GOD FATHER = GOD LOVE = GOD HOLY SPIRIT
created the human spirit in His own image

Primordial Spiritual
----------Creation

**HUMAN
SPIRIT**

Secondary Spiritual
----------Creation

Sphere of Animistic
----Substantiality

-Ethereal World

**CASCADE OF WAVE CONVERTERS
(SPEED REDUCTION)**

-----Astral World

CHAKRAS

**Spectrum of the
dissected White Light**

-------------World
of Matter
(Physical World)

Ill.10

At the level of the Astral World, the waves start to dissect into a spectrum. Indians once called this spectrum "chakras", which is translated as "wheels", but instead they are rays of light. Thus, our body assimilates the already dissected White Light and not the full stream of Light. This assimilation is the point of dissection into the spectrum.

Love comes from the spirit, which is Light, Love, and Will. But if it is clutched at the astral level with our sins, we receive only a drip: a little bit of love, a little bit of creative ability. Some people get more of it than others. And what if we break through our sins? The result is a waterfall of Love and Light! But who will give it to us in our present state? That means someone has to come here and *ignite* our souls. Thus, a mediator is needed who will come and deliver that spark on Earth. That is why God sent *the Second One*. He arrived and now gives it out. Take it! And I received it from that source in 1994. I became ignited and I started moving. But I was required to learn everything on my own. When the going gets tough, help comes. But in training mode, there is no help. Deal with it, be patient, keep working! That is how you edify yourself.

In the first few weeks of my struggle on this road, I was given a bonus, and I took it as a gift. It was amazing! Two, three weeks went by, and I became a clairvoyant. I solved a crime and helped my friend whose apartment was robbed. I received the names of the thieves and some other information. I was astonished by my abilities, thinking how great I was! I became so conceited! Back then, I was still full of vanity. It was just bursting out of me! And suddenly, I made a mistake in my detective work. I said, "Why? I thought this information was correct." I received this answer: "Do you want to live off of handouts all the time? It was given to you so that you would believe and strengthen your faith. Now, get back down to earth and start from scratch." Of course, I became disheartened. And there I thought of how easily I became so great. It turns out, I must build the building - my Temple! I was shown the Light and the Way. So I went, and joy came! Now, get down to earth and start building. I was shown a few things in advance, but I must build the Temple myself.

In the end, it's not God who will take the test for you, like in some corrupt establishment where the teacher grades you for money. It doesn't work that way! The Law is very strict and stern. The Law requires us, who were null in spirit, to now get up and start building the Temple. And I managed to build it to a certain extent. It's not completed yet, but the construction continues. Little by little, stones are adding together.

22. SHAME AND CHASTITY

The road to freedom from sin is far from easy. Often, errors are made along the way. You roll back, realize your mistakes, and feel ashamed, thinking to yourself, "If there is shame, there is still a conscience inside." Conscience reacts this way. When there is no conscience left, there is no shame either. When I see esotericism insist that it is necessary to fight shame, I say - nonsense! *Shame is the foundation of chastity*. There is a victory of spirit over sin inherent in shame.

Where does the conscience come from? Conscience is a signal of the discrepancy between the main wave from God that created us, the human spirit, and something we did wrong, or thought wrong, or said wrong. Why do you feel ashamed? Because your wave does not correspond to the wave of your Parent and, in fact, to you in spirit. Conscience is telling you, "This is not yours; why are you acting this way?" So, the prosecutor's supervision appears within, and you feel bad, you feel ashamed. If this supervision is still alive, then the person is still alive, meaning his soul is still alive. That person can still have accomplishments.

Abd-Ru-Shin writes in the chapter "Chastity" of how people misinterpret the meaning of it. Most people think that virginity and celibacy are the essences of chastity. Not at all! It depends on what consciousness puts into it.

Some people abandoned intimate life and were dubbed saints on Earth. This act is a terrible foolishness! God said, and it is written in the Old Testament, "God blessed them and said to them, 'Be fruitful and increase in number'..." (Genesis, 1:28). This right was given to you. Live in joy. But *love* each other. If you love a person you are with, there is no sin in intimacy. *If you don't love each other, you will always commit a sin*. Even if you have a marriage certificate and are wedded twenty times in all religions of the world, you will still be sinners, because you do not live in love. ***An intimate relationship without love is adultery.*** That is all.

Abd-Ru-Shin writes that chastity isn't the rejection of basic life pleasures, only just like everything else, those pleasures should be experienced in moderation. You must first love each other. And if you reject intimate life, what is your goal? If you genuinely have dedicated your life to God, and you are a passionary who just has no time for it, then perhaps it's a valid reason. Even so, why deprive yourself of these colors of life? However, when you want to be known as a saint, which is a terrible vanity, and try to pose as a righteous celibate, this becomes an awful distortion! You are harming your body and, additionally, creating a false image. Because your body is given to you for this purpose also, and you must live fully.

Surprisingly, people found a way to create an unhealthy commotion around the sexual component of human relations. Just think of how we perceive intimate relationships. Nearly all cuss words revolve around sexual relationships! What gives color to these words? Not that the words themselves are bad, but that the person *believes* that it is bad, it is an insult. If a child hears these words for the first time and they are expressed without a hint of insult or anger, he will not consider them bad or sinful.

There is no sin in sexual relationships given that a man and a woman *love* each other.

23. RESENTMENT IS JUDGMENT

If God came to save this world, He came to save only those who are focused on Him and move towards Him. And of those who have no interest or faith in it, God says, "Well, leave the trial to Me". It's in the Bible: "It is mine to avenge; I will repay." (Romans, 12:19). Those people will meet their fate when the time is right. You have no authority to judge them. "Do not judge, or you too will be judged." (Matthew, 7:1). But you *do* judge, day and night. ***Your resentment and complaints to this world are your judgment.***

When you demand justice immediately, here and now, that is your vindictiveness. The thought "I want this person to suffer, because he made me suffer!" *is* judgment! How is this different from analyzing? On the surface, it might seem that I am also judging them, one after another. I say, this is not judging but analyzing. Analyzing and judging are two different things. Not only do we have the right to analyze, but we *must* do it! First, my soul makes a moral assessment: I like this, and I don't like that. Then, I must explain to my brain why I don't like a particular situation or a person who created it. Maybe because that person is a loud, hostile, and mean creature. But I don't want him to suffer, even though he is a thief, crook, or a brawler. There is the role of the Supervisor, the chief Prosecutor. *He* will repay. My goal is to lead my soul out of this negative influence, to not be offended or frustrated. That is the first victory. The second goal is to do something for those affected by that person's actions. So, first is not allowing yourself into a state of frustration and, when you have learned how to do it, you may teach others. Then other people will react in the right way too. Thus, the brawlers won't agitate them. People will just perceive them with a certain degree of humor, which is one of the greatest weapons against negativity.

When I trained people, I used to say, "While you are still weak and can't resist negativity, play this game: imagine every morning you get out of bed and step into this world. There are people in white coats - normal people, doctors - and there are mental patients. You are on the grounds of a psychiatric ward. This world is already a real mental asylum. Thus, you must react accordingly. Currently, your reaction towards them is the same as it is to normal people. When you get offended, it means you expected a regular interaction with a reasonable, intelligent person. Suppose you walked by and lightly touched him with your elbow, and he cursed you out. Your natural reaction is to feel insulted! But you thought he was normal, and he isn't. He merely wears a mask of being friendly and polite. He might even know the Bible, Socrates, and every Prophet or philosopher by heart. But it all lingers in his head, not touching the soul. Thus, he only *seems* intelligent. So, you got offended, and that is wrong. Instead, you must instantly forgive him. Then the Law comes into effect. It will punish him quickly enough. Otherwise, your negative reaction will form the otherworldly astral binds with him. Thus, you become *chained* to him. And until you break those ties *by forgiveness*, you will be dragged in this harness with the rest of the crowd into the abyss."

In order to separate yourself, you must learn to forgive, to not be afraid, and to not be provoked by any other negative emotion. Only then you cut off all the "vines" and start taking off! Your balloon is free. Depart. The Bible calls this process the separation of sheep from the goats. "All the nations will be gathered before him, and he will separate the people one from another as a shepherd separates the sheep from the goats. He will put the sheep on his right and the goats on his left." (Matthew, 25:32-33). When the sheep step aside, God says, "I will have My Justice! But first, you must step aside. Otherwise, how do I judge the whole crowd? I need to take out the part that is focused on rectification. I will help them." But the bulk who are described as "many are invited, but few are chosen" (Matthew, 22:14), the unchosen ones, will be dealt with by God after you separate. The grain is removed from the rocks. The useful remains, the useless will be destroyed. There is justice in that. The process is described in the Bible and repeated in *In the Light of Truth* at the modern level.

24. WHAT IS DISEASE?

Let's look at the human body. Hardly anyone can brag that absolutely nothing ever hurts. As doctors say, "There are no healthy people, only underdiagnosed ones." So, what is a disease, and why do people become ill?

A human body is made of cells. We are all familiar with cytology, the life of a cell, at least at the school-level anatomy. There are cytoplasm, mitochondria, and other cellular components. The cell is what assembles our liver, lungs, nerves, and other tissue. The cell is made of atoms, which is a scientific fact, and not one materialist can deny it. And what is an atom? Let's take the basic atom with two electrons charged (-1) each, two neutrons with no electric charge, and two protons with a positive electric charge. Assuming this is an ideal atom, centrifugal and centripetal forces are equalized everywhere, meaning electrons spin ideally on all their orbits. Intra-nuclear relations are also ideally balanced. Due to what factor are all atomic structures balanced, and the entire system is sustained at rest and in perfect order? Due to the wave speed of C = 300,000 km/sec. Matter doesn't have any other wave. This speed is the *balancing force*. And what is the destabilizing factor? As I have said before: 400C.

If I throw this chalk at the wall with all my strength, it will shatter into pieces. What happens to the wall? There won't be much damage. But if I load this mass into a high caliber rifle and shoot at the wall, there will be a hole in the wall. If we launch it out of a cannon, it will utterly smash the wall. And if we hurl it with rocket speed, I don't know what we will have. So, the speed makes a colossal difference when dealing with the same mass - same mass, but different speed.

A similar principle applies to the impact of impulses, our emotions. Emotion has a speed higher than the speed of light C, where C is what keeps everything balanced in physical matter. Take such emotions or feelings as fear, jealousy, grievance, irritability, or envy. When these waves strike, naturally, matter cannot withstand the blow because these emotions have a higher speed. Then all electrons get swept away from their usual paths. If the amplitude of these emotions is strong, it reaches the intra-nuclear structure and impairs the intra-nuclear balance. As a result, the atom becomes distorted. Naturally, a cell comprised of such atoms begins to crush at the biochemical level. Then the cell sustainability (its respiration) is disturbed, i.e., the waste isn't taken out promptly, and the nutrients aren't taken in. It is called disturbance of metabolism – the beginning of a disease. When the initially perfectly healthy cell is under a constant disruption, it eventually becomes permanently altered. Look at your life – it is a continuous sequence of fears, grievances, and other negativity. It's our reaction to this world. We live in a state of the permanent search for justice, but we cannot find it because we ourselves aren't just. And mistakenly, we start blazing with negative emotions. They are called "negative" because they *negate* God's Will. *They are not in accordance with God's Will, so it is a sin.*

After explaining this to myself, I got rid of them. Not because I forbade myself to feel negative emotions, but because I realized I was battling with God. And you cannot fight God. I wanted to be healthy and happy, and I became such. *For that, you must live by the Law.*

Thus, when fear, irritability, grievances, and jealousy died, my atoms slowly restored to balance. Cells made of these atoms, consequently, stopped suffering. The cells of my liver, joints, and everything else came to a norm. What is there so difficult or miraculous? It's nothing special. That is what a disease is. *It is a result of our unwillingness to live by the Laws of God.*

And how do I help others? If a person's cells or atoms are in distress, my spiritual system starts transferring waves through the line of calmness. I take him "under my wing" with my soul. Let's say he is sick, or perhaps he is my student who has suffered, and now he has negative matrixes in his field, which need to be destroyed. If his soul is yet unable to repel the attacks at the astral and physical levels, then I cover him with my soul and start straightening things out. My stronger vibrations start covering him, amending the situation at the level of his field. When a repair occurs at the level of the field, cells start receiving normal, stabilizing subsidy of energy. The formula $E=MC^2$ reflects this phenomenon from the scientific point of view. I.e., my energy E is in abundance, and by transmitting it, I eventually start forming normal matter. I get regular, stabilizing flow through the line of *right* energy. That is how the extrasensory psychics work. Only not every psychic is made equal.

The overwhelming majority of extrasensory psychics and various "energy healers" have tapped into the Astral World, where the wave speed of energy is 400C. This realm is where they draw their "healing powers" from. Only 1 out of 1000 or even 10,000 people takes it from the spiritual source and the rest of the 9,999, from the Astral World. If one operates out of the astral, he does nothing but harm. He can correct your cells because he uses a higher speed – 400C. But if he doesn't live by the Laws, his field is speckled with specific matrixes – attachment to the astral lie, *which is the form of demons*. Then, when he corrects your cells, together with the temporary retreat of a physical illness, the patient gets distortions and matrixes which are coming from the psychic into the patient's astral field and down to his physical level. And later, the psychic can no longer remove those harmful matrixes even if he wants to. Because a wave of a stronger one is needed to "melt" them, which he doesn't possess. The melting temperature must reach *the spiritual height* in order to dissolve it. I had many people come to me with this phenomenon after visiting psychics. I remove it little by little, and their condition slowly stabilizes. Although, at first, as I said, the work of those "healers" seems to be helping. But later, after the health improvement, one gets a phenomenon of the worst order. Thus, watch who you can and can't trust. The sources are different. Once again, the Astral World has pretty strong waves, but they are, unfortunately, impure.

When you open up to a healer operating with the astral waves, the true nature of the man that didn't master the Commandment carries into your field. How do you open up? By *trusting* that person: "I am here, heal me, I want it, I am tired of being sick." Thus, you open up your soul, therefore breaking the Commandment. What did God say? "I am the Lord your God… you shall have no other gods before Me…" (Exodus, 20:2-3). Meaning, you shall not make idols. Because you can trust only God. At least, read a prayer before going to see someone that you presume to trust. Pray deeply to the Lord's Prayer, maybe even three times. Say, "God, if there is harm, deliver me from temptation, deliver me from evil." Then the situation itself will prompt you. Maybe you'll see that the trip doesn't come together. What is diverting you from it? God is! Since you can't hear Him, you start getting "silent" obstacles. Read your life! You prayed and asked for help, and you are receiving it. You are being delivered from evil.

Since we touched upon the Lord's Prayer, let's discuss the meaning of it. You can find the full Prayer in the Gospel of Matthew 6:9-13. This Prayer is very powerful and helpful. It helped me as well, especially at the beginning of my spiritual work. The Prayer starts "Our Father in Heaven" so, I accept with my soul that there is God in Heaven. "Hallowed be Your name" - I see images of the Light burning brighter. I won't go over the entire Prayer. The phrase "And forgive us our debts, as we also have forgiven our debtors" is quite interesting. When one doesn't know how to forgive, he forgives only verbally, but he is hurting on the inside. So, the grievance is still there, which is registered Up Above. Then, he is told "How *you* forgive, *in the same way* you will be forgiven." If you are saying, "Forgive *us* our debts, *as we* also have forgiven our debtors," but there is no true forgiveness within you, then you are not forgiven either. The Prayer holds the condition on which your sins are forgiven to you! *God will forgive you if you yourself will forgive others.* As you see, *humility is embedded in the Law.* Jesus gave us a very profound Prayer, indeed. It contains everything we need to know.

"*Avert us* from temptation but deliver us from the evil one." Although it is written "<u>Lead us not</u> into temptation but deliver us from the evil one," but in the Bible, it is also written "For God cannot be tempted by evil, nor does He tempt anyone." (James, 1:13). Thus, a mistake has been made in the interpretation. The translation is incorrect. Instead, it should say "*Avert us* from temptation," meaning help us not to be tempted. It is very logical and straightforward. In other words, you may also say, "I am yet a very weak Christian, I just started this journey. I don't have enough strength to fight off demons. *Avert* me from temptation, deliver me from the evil one." Do you see how meaningful this is? The words "lead us not into temptation" are rather odd. For God doesn't lead into temptation! A demon does! So, the translations are inaccurate.

Back in 1994, when I started applying the concept of living by the Laws, I set a strict guideline: no medicine and no doctors, regardless of what hurts or how much it hurts; I won't help myself. I had to test whether this system really works. In the beginning, I would get very ill with a high fever. In the first 7–8 months, I had to deal with four major illnesses; after that, there were less and less. I was defeating them without any medicine, and my recovery was much faster. For example, a strong case of bronchitis took me 2–3 days to overcome. If it came together with the flu, recovery time was a maximum of 7–8 days. You understand what the flu is together with bronchitis: it feels like your bones are breaking.

My daughter is a doctor. She would say, "Let me give you a shot!" She felt sorry for me. It hurt her to see me in pain. My response always was, "No. I have to bear it on my own." Why was I so adamant about it? Because if I am supposed to be ill, I must endure it, *for I believe that my suffering is a response from my past wrongful behavior before the Law.* I don't want to shield myself from God, from His Law, with a pill. If it is meant for me to have severe pain, I must bear it. *But this doesn't mean all of you must do the same.*

At times people call me, saying, "Oh, I've committed a terrible sin – I took medicine!" I say, "Why are you repenting to me? You simply couldn't resist the pain. So, you took a pill, what's so unusual? Besides, no need to repent to me when there is God. You will sort it out with Him. I can only explain things to you and help you, but you keep the record before the Law, not before me." Do not repent to me. I don't forbid you to take medicine. Take it regularly if you wish; that's not a problem. I have only described *my* experience. I purposely gave myself a more rigorous regimen. That is why I've progressed so fast in spirit. I decided "all or nothing" - I will either die or break through. I made that choice. I thought I was living a good life: I had love, I nearly went through war, I experienced many things. It was plenty. If I died now, that's ok; so I went "all in". That meant I conquered fear, for I no longer feared death. Not everyone can immediately achieve this, but I did. While you still have fear, there will always be the thought: "What if I die?! I can die if I don't take medicine. I'm running a fever over 104 F!" In this case, do as your soul desires. If you want to take medicine, do it. There is no big sin in it. You'll only slow down the process of redemption. Once you get stronger, you'll continue on this road. Not everyone is able to handle "maximum mode". There is no coercion in it, for we have full freedom of choice. The main goal is to conquer laziness and to figure out what's stopping you from committing to this venture – laziness or the feeling of uselessness of this matter.

Throughout the years of working with people, I've concluded that ailing health is one of the leading reasons to start searching for answers beyond one's medicine cabinet. Physical pain is a huge motivator, and the question "How do I become healthy?" concerns most of the population. As I said earlier, to maintain perfect health, we must obey the Laws of God. Our deviations from the Laws are mainly emotional. That includes fear, jealousy, envy, despondency, resentment, irritability, and anger - the highest phase of irritability. Perhaps, there are some other emotions and their combinations, but we will keep it simple.

Each emotion has its own type of radiation. At first, I perceived those emotions as a whole, like something unpleasant. Later, with experience, I learned to discern the "taste" of resentment, the taste of jealousy or its radiation, etc. Just like any radiation, one slightly differs from the other. It is hard to explain. For example, you can describe the taste of cake. Candy tastes similar, also sweet and delicious, but in a different way. How do we describe this difference and express it in earthly concepts? It's not easy, as with negative emotions. Each one is harmful in its own way. These "tonalities" helped me in the past to figure out different life circumstances, diseases, and fates, when I worked with people. Each emotion is tied to a specific neural center of the body. For instance, pride and vanity mostly affect the throat and the associated organs. Irritability and despondency also strike this area, often affecting the heart region as well. In the meantime, our brain is *always* involved.

When I do a healing session with a person having health problems, I see that their brain is always darkened. The brain includes the hypothalamus, thalamus, pituitary, medulla oblongata, frontal lobe, etc. All these structures form our behavior. If we let our brain alone shape our behavior, it will lead us to frequent mistakes because our brain isn't the Truth. It is an intermediate stage. But we let the enemy invade our territory. Who is our enemy? *It's the emotions we have created.* Those forms are alive and resemble spots. Our ancestors called them demons, and advanced modern science calls them "solitons". They are clusters of energy that tend to move, hide, and act as if they are living entities; only they are otherworldly. They are also known as "ghosts" or "phantoms". I won't get into details, but the fact is that they exist and lead us to disease and trouble.

Thus, we can say that *our diseases are the demons that surround us*. And we are the ones who've created those demons. By the Law of Justice of this world, you can't be affected by someone else's demons. Your own demons are plenty. "A man reaps what he sows" (Galatians, 6:7). Count how many times a day you are mistaken and multiply it by the years of life (and not just one life). That whole group of demons is dragging behind you, *and there is only one way to get rid of it*. I am not the one who came up with this method. I merely used it, without even realizing it at first. Later, I recognized it when I read it in the Bible! "Forgive, and you will be forgiven." (Luke, 6:37). "For if you forgive other people when they sin against you, your Heavenly Father will also forgive you. But if you do not forgive others their sins, your Father will not forgive your sins." (Matthew, 6:14-15). Jesus said so!

25. CHAKRAS
AND ENERGY SUPPLY OF THE BODY

Chakras is what the Indians once called the otherworldly energy supply for each neural plexus of our physical body. There is the sacral plexus, lumbar, solar, chest area, cervical, pituitary region (the brain), and, finally, one beyond the physical body. It is a spectrum of light, which the Indians saw in the Astral World (Illustration 10). The White Light that comes from the Source contains the whole spectrum of light. We know this from physics. With the growing distance, the White Light eventually loses Its power and adhesion, and channels off into the spectrum at the level of the Astral World. This spectrum has seven colors. Each of these colored lights is responsible for certain processes.

I will give you a few examples of common ailments and explain why they occur in our bodies. For instance, take nail fungus. Our feet receive their supply of energy from the sacral plexus. And the sacral plexus is tied to what the Indians call the 1st chakra. It is the 1st ray of the spectrum, which has the red energy of radiation, supplying our legs and feet. So, why do feet suffer? Because the red sacral plexus isn't working properly. It is weak and not transmitting the nerve signals, which happens when the sacral plexus doesn't receive any energy subsidy from the red ray. And the red ray corresponds to the *spiritual agility*. If one is spiritually inactive, the 1st chakra shuts down. As a result, energy in the legs stops circulating, and disease takes place in the legs and joints, such as arthritis and similar ailments. Also, the lower area of the body becomes vulnerable, and the musculoskeletal system will suffer along with other organs connected to the bottom level. In order to improve the health of the legs and feet, one must spur his spirituality, i.e., evolve faster in spirit. I had heavy legs together with spinal problems. After only four months of amending myself, I forgot all about my spine. It became rubber-like. My legs received an impulse, and the energy meridians opened up. So, the 1st chakra is always damaged if a person is spiritually lazy. Usually, the entire spine, which is a part of the central nervous system (the brain and the spinal cord), will bear a negative impact. Nowadays, it is rare to see someone with a healthy back, even among young people.

The 2nd chakra often suffers due to the wrong relationships between a man and a woman, a child and a parent, or between friends. Feminine selfishness and male egoism strike the pelvic region – the 2nd chakra. Also, envy affects this chakra. That is, if a man is envious of another man's talent or charisma, or a woman is envious of another woman's beauty or other attributes.

However, material envy strikes the 3rd chakra, which is located at the level of the solar plexus. Materialism and greed, along with a strong attachment to earthly possessions, affect it as well. Many might ask, "What's wrong with striving for a better life?" Nothing, of course! But, at the same time, we must not forget our origin – the Spiritual World. Those who have forgotten and refuse to realize it will suffer. But that is their choice. Also, this chakra becomes blocked if one has fears. Fears can manifest in a variety of ways. After all, greed is also a fear. It is when one is afraid to run out of money, so he won't lend it to anyone; he would rather bury it or hide it away. One is fearful of what tomorrow might bring and thinks money will help him to stay afloat. This pathology, ultimately, is also a product of fear. Fears are very diverse if you try to sort them out. Thus, the solar plexus is where all the material hang-ups strike us.

The 4th chakra (the heart region) suffers if a woman lacks femininity and a man, masculinity. That's when a person is "dull". This chakra also harbors anger and jealousy. Additionally, a tendency to cruelty and many other deviations undermine it.

The 5th chakra (throat) holds grievances, vanity, hopelessness, anger, and selfishness. These emotions also affect our heart. The throat is impacted if a person is very resentful or arrogant, resulting in thyroid problems. The thyroid is majorly responsible for our immunity. Next to the thyroid gland, we have two pairs of parathyroid glands responsible for the water-salt balance. When there is a system malfunction, the excess salts might accumulate and precipitate in our body, such as our neck, knees, and other joints. Or we experience the opposite – lack of salts. They are washed out if we have excess water. Then we get edema, and our bone tissue suffers, becoming brittle. Thus, both conditions are bad. An ideal balance is needed, the middle, *the norm.*

The 6th chakra is our head. Energy supply at this level becomes altered due to all sorts of "isms" taking over one's consciousness: materialism, fanaticism, nationalism, fundamentalism, and so on. Any *false* concept is considered an "ism". Those are the lies that have entrapped us through our heads and now rule over our thinking. *Ultimately, these wrong ideas control us*. We made *intellect* our chief commander, *forgetting about the soul*. Thus, our brain, as our commander, begins to suffer. And it is well deserved. If your computer gets a virus like a Trojan, you know what happens next: it disrupts all the programs, and the computer crashes. The same "Trojan" now sits in our heads, ever since the Fall of Man. It is very strong, and its power is rising. So, thanks to this virus, we have received the life we have now. From a health perspective, the blockage of the 6th chakra leads to bad vessels, improperly functioning pituitary gland, and hypothalamus not producing the right hormones. Then our thyroid doesn't get the thyroid-stimulating hormone, and the secondary hormones aren't produced. The adrenals aren't getting the corticotrophin, causing renal insufficiency. Where do all of these problems start? *In our head,* just like the old saying. Because our head is our commander, you see.

The 7th chakra is out-of-body. To be honest, I don't fully understand the role of this chakra. But I know that when it is blocked, one suffers from migraines. Migraines start when the 1st and 7th chakras become blocked. The 1st one is blocked due to our spiritual laziness and the 7th – I don't know why. Then, the whole person is "clogged", as the energy current is interrupted.

The system of energy circulation throughout the human body is very vast! Man has the energy meridians (as in Chinese medicine), which resemble Earth's power lines, only our system is much more complicated. The Lines of Force act in both directions, meaning the reciprocal flows of Light take place. If the 1st and the 7th chakras are gridlocked, the flow of energy is disturbed, and the person becomes sick. Migraines and other ailments start happening, including terrible mood swings. So, when you remove all that is blocking the energy supply to your body, the meridians open up and resume the regular flow of energy throughout the body.

A person must breathe energetically. If all chakras are open, the Light then arrives undistorted and in abundance. Thus, we receive a complete spectrum of support from Above. However, only an ideal person can consistently maintain this scenario. For us to receive an undisrupted flow of energy, we must keep ourselves in a perfect balance, the norm. And what is the norm? Stop being resentful, selfish, greedy, fearful, frustrated, angry, and so on. Accelerate in spirit! You must evolve quickly. Straighten out your relationship with the opposite sex. Women cannot blame their partners for everything and vice versa. As many commonly say, "You ruined my life! I devoted the best years of my life to you." Or "I earn money; what else do you want from me?" Those stereotypical dialogs happen everywhere, regardless of a geographical location, social status, or level of income. But can we really measure a man solely by how much money he makes or by his devotion to his family?

I speak to many women, and some say their husbands are, indeed, the perfect family men. However, they feel stagnation, boredom, and stuffiness of the world. A woman wants something vivid, bright, and exciting from her man. But he doesn't have it. So, she goes to a rebellious drifter, and she is happy with him. Why does this happen? I say because one man has this quality, another one has another quality, the third one has something else, and so on. The same thing is with women. Everyone has something to offer. And we want to gather it all, wishing to find everything in one person. But such a woman or such a man needs to be raised, *which comes from following the Commandments.*

So, when a person conquers spiritual laziness, learns healthy relationships, eliminates envy, greed, materialism, and other wrong emotions, he himself clears his way upward. We are the ones who have buried ourselves, and our goal is to start digging ourselves out.

26. COMBATING NEGATIVE EMOTIONS

It is important to know that in the difficult process of eliminating negative emotions, there is no one-size-fits-all solution. *Each specific emotion needs a different approach.* I will give you a few tools for combating the most common negative emotions that rule over us: fear, irritability, resentment, greed, envy, and jealousy.

Fear was the easiest emotion for me to extinguish. I am not talking about an instinct of self-preservation, but of our many various unfounded fears and paranoia. ***Fear is conquered by faith.*** When you possess true faith and are in the state of Connection, i.e., the real baptism took place, while actively working on reducing your demons in the form of negative character traits, you can be assured of the protection by the Will of God from the Darkside. Dark forces are *finite*. They are limited by the material boundaries – the physical and the out-worldly astral (the realm of the medium gross matter). Beyond that, the Pure World begins. And far beyond that is the Giant – *the Infinity of God's Will*. For God's Will to destroy this tiny patch of the Darkness is a small task. In my battle with fear, I told myself, "God is Perfection; He is the Highest Power; thus, any finite value is infinitely small compared to Infinity. Then what is there to be afraid of if God is with me? If I possess real faith, and I am overcoming my demons while being supported by the Will of God, then nothing can harm me. I am under the Highest Protection!" That is how all my fears died. I have the certainty that God is stronger than the Darkside. Only God must be with you and you with God. Then, there is nothing to be afraid of. That is all.

Another prevalent emotion is *irritability*. This emotion has several stages: dissatisfaction, annoyance, frustration, and anger, which is the highest degree of irritability. Irritability is very similar to resentment. We become irritated with people on almost a daily basis. It may be a child, a neighbor, a coworker, a driver on the road, or someone else. How do we eliminate this emotion? I managed to destroy my first irritability by taking a simple approach. I went out in the city - those were my early days of spiritual work. I took the subway in Moscow, which is always very crowded, people rushing and hustling. I was also in a hurry because I had to be somewhere on time, and I don't like to be late. All that bumping into people was getting on my nerves, and I started becoming annoyed. On the surface, I was composing myself, but on the inside, I was bothered by the crowd. I became irritated.

As I got home, I started analyzing what had happened. Why did I get irritated? Because I was bumping into people, it was too crowded. Why was I bumping into them? Because I was in a rush as I didn't want to be late. Why was I in a rush? Because I had to be on time. But to be on time was *my* goal. Other people had to be somewhere too. Somebody was picking up a child, or going to work, or some grandma was going to the market. Why wasn't I taking *their* interests into consideration? They were also in a rush. I don't own the city, we all share it, right? So, was it selfish of me? Yes, it was! Besides, I was late because I didn't plan my day accordingly. If I had left 10 minutes earlier, I could have used that extra time and calmly maneuver to avoid any obstacles. I would have had the time, instead of impatiently looking at my watch. Whose fault was it that I didn't plan my day right and put my interests before the interests of those around me? It was my fault! Thus, as a decent and honest man, I shouldn't have been irritated but instead apologized to the people I bumped into.

Consequently, my irritability started dying when I had to deal with public transportation. Now, when I have to be in crowded places like the subway or a train station, I tell myself, "My schedule is market – railway station, that's it." I must gather all my patience and go in like a rugby offense. So, I got myself together and became "thicker", so to speak. That's how I defeated my first burst of temper. And we must conquer it each time it tries to take over us, because it will. Life continually presents a variety of situations that provoke us to become annoyed, frustrated, irritated, or angry.

Resentment, or feeling offended, is similar to irritability. *We deserve everything this world presents to us*, and we must accept it without evil because irritability and feeling offended are also evil. How do we combat resentment? It has been said: if you can't change the world, change your perception of it. The way I changed my perception was that *I began to see this world based on the knowledge of the Laws*. The Law of Freedom of Choice ensures that everyone chooses their own model of behavior. Whether it's a villain, a corrupt official, or yet another pseudo-missionary who is trying to spread the word of the so-called "Truth", that is their choice! They think this is normal. They team up in some social or political groups protected by earthly laws. But there is no need to start that battle. Leave them to their conviction, for their conscience is no longer their guide. They have that right by the Law of Freedom of Choice. *And we must respect the Law of God!* Our psyche - our "I", our consciousness, is in our hands. *If you want to create a better life, then get yourself together and start doing what Jesus said.*

Let's look at _greed_. For greed to be harmful, it doesn't have to be expressed to a degree of pathology, such as "I won't share anything with anyone." Attachment to material matter is also considered greed; it is when one is fully consumed by money-making, fancy furniture, good cars, and other material possessions. Their goal is to attain social status and to possess more than their neighbor. That is a dead-end road. No matter how much one has, it's never enough because there is always someone who has more. So, the competition is permanent. And if one doesn't win that race, he becomes envious. To defeat greed, we must set our priorities straight. **Our spiritual goal must prevail over any earthly goals.** Jesus said, "For where your treasure is, there your heart will be also." (Matthew, 6:21). My soul is of the utmost importance to me, and I always keep that in mind.

Envy is a very prevalent emotion, and it comes from a desire to possess. The desire itself isn't harmful. The harm comes from the thought: if one has something I don't, then I don't want him to have it either. When someone is envious, he releases a demon that leads to misfortunes for the other person. We must have a deep understanding of this. What happens when a person is envious of the other, or a group of people? *That person creates and releases the "dark spots" (demons), which by the Law of Resemblance attract similar spots a hundredfold and come back to crush him.* That means he himself is ruining his life, killing any luck, and becoming even more envious. Because he is suffering, and his neighbor isn't. Envy is well described in classical literature, such as Jack London's *Moon-Face*. In it, one character tried to poison his neighbor's garden by sprinkling salt on the soil. Eventually, he poisoned everything and still did not attain peace.

If you want to own something, you must strive for it! Get to work, don't be lazy, _earn it_! And if it is not achievable at the moment, *accept it with humility.* **For we deserve everything that each day brings to us.** Essentially, *envy is an expression of non-humility.* One is not happy with their status, or their car, or their house. Or he might not be as talented as his neighbor, or he might not be as spiritually evolved as the next guy. Someone might have a more attractive wife, while the other – healthier children, the list goes on. There are many factors that cause envy. To conquer it, one must tell oneself, "What I have today is what I have earned according to the Law of Retribution." If there is something you weren't given today, try to get it tomorrow or the day after. How? *Change yourself for the better.* The more good you put out there, the more fortunate your life will become. Don't chase that fortune away with your mistakes. It is that simple. For true religion, including Christianity, is absolute simplicity.

Next, let's look at *jealousy*. I briefly touched on this emotion in the chapter "Heavenly Love". Jealousy is an interesting quality and very difficult to extinguish. Jealousy was never a spawning of love. If a man loves somebody and becomes jealous, he is only tormented by this negative emotion. He can feel hurt because he is losing his loved one. He is sad and hurt, but, at the same time, if he truly loves, he never wishes anything bad for that person. Jealousy is an indicator of emitting negative emotions, so it becomes sickening to be around that person, even if he is silent.

Take domestic jealousy. Maybe a person is late from work. Their spouse doesn't know why they are late, but suspicion is already there, which creates a dysfunctional atmosphere at home. The astral waves are hovering over both of them. It is their mutual field, and neither one can escape it. Thus, when we have such a toxic atmosphere at home, we are suffering and wondering why. When you are loved and respected, you feel it. You feel good around that person. But when you are pressed by negative emotions, you feel uncomfortable. If a person is moody and jealous, the emotions are silent, but they are active. ***Emotion is also action!***

Therefore, jealousy is a spawn of egoism. Once again, if I love a woman, I shouldn't perceive her as my possession. A woman is not a suitcase that you can put where you want. She also has freedom and personal interests. It doesn't matter whether you love her or not. She is an individual! When you start understanding this, you learn the Law of Freedom of Choice. Suppose a woman I love left me for another man. If I love *her* (I accentuate that *I love her* and not *me*), then I must say, "My love, I am crying, but I want you to be happy, even if it means you must be with another man. If you found someone more deserving, I am happy for you. I proved to be a weak partner for you." That's it. It is painful to accept, but you must if you love somebody. However, if you love *yourself,* you will love in a different way: "How dare you leave *me*? You betrayed me! You are no good!"

Love in the family cannot be invented. It isn't a product of thinking. Love is either there or it isn't. So, it's quite silly to demand love from one who doesn't have it, or when a person has cooled off towards you. You have to accept it calmly because when a separation happens, there is a reason to be self-critical. If a woman is leaving me, that means I must take a good look at *myself* instead of her or her new partner. Maybe if I look at him, I will see that he is a much more interesting person than I am. Why not admit it? If you are free from vanity, you will accept it. If you don't have envy and jealousy, you might say, "In order to catch up with him and have a chance to win her back, not only do I need to catch up but to outrun him. What are the good qualities he possesses?" You start thinking, "My body is pretty fit, no problem there. Then take intellect: I'm not a downer, and I am a well-educated person. I can discuss music, theater, play the guitar, sing, and even write poetry. What about my spirit?" If spiritually a man is a pigmy and a woman is evolved and keeps on growing, of course she will slowly grow distant from him! That is what sometimes happens in families that took the route of spiritual evolution. It is great when both husband and wife grow together hand in hand. But when a woman starts spiritually growing, very often her husband rebels: "You must choose between me and this cult!" I say, "Bring him. Let him hear the lecture and judge for himself what kind of cult this is. If he takes it on, he will also benefit from it, and his life will blossom." But often they adamantly refuse to even consider the possibility of listening or reading anything of the sort. Sometimes they get so stubborn that it leads to divorce. There have been many cases like that.

If things are relatively calm in the family, and a woman starts moving upward but her husband doesn't, the gap between them grows ever bigger. It's even noticeable in intellect when one is intellectually growing, and their partner isn't. It leads to one becoming uninteresting to another because we must always be learning something new.

The bottom line is, we must get rid of jealousy. We have the right to be heartbroken if a person chooses to leave, but we have no authority over them. When it comes to a relationship, there is no such thing as entitlement. We cannot force someone to love us, demanding their undivided attention. *We must deserve it and earn it daily.*

Since we touched upon the subject of a man/woman relationship, let's discuss what makes the foundation for a happy couple. In my conversations with men, I often notice that men perceive women, first of all, as sexual partners and, secondly, as domestic servants - two components. I say, why can't we see a woman simply as a person who is, by the way, much more abundant than us men? Women have that unique "zest" men lack. A woman has a very abundant inner world *if she has preserved her femininity*. If a woman retains that inner beauty and strength of her soul, she can give a lot to a man.

Abd-Ru-Shin writes that a man can only reach a certain height in the Spiritual World, and that is his limit, whereas a woman has one link to the Higher World – the World of Primordial Beings. That World is faster and more beautiful. That is where a woman gets her charm from. This charm comes into this world and conquers men. But if a woman becomes rough and crude, starts following trends, showing off, flirting, and putting her body on display, she turns into a "shallow beauty", slowly loses her femininity, and stops being a *woman*. In turn, a man stops being a *man* when he no longer wants to protect her feminine beauty, respect her, and take care of her. He stops being a man in the true sense of the word. Then all that is left is his "man costume". Our appropriate attire is not what makes us a man or a woman. Gender begins Up Higher, in the Heavens. Abd-Ru-Shin writes about it, explaining the moment with Adam and Eve, and the proverbial rib. He writes of how the gender split happened. Because beyond the Spiritual World, there is no gender. Up There, there is only one ray of Light. We have been separated here on purpose. But that topic won't be covered in this book.

So, if a woman continues to cultivate her pure femininity and we, men, develop our male hypostasis, only good will come out of it. But when a man assumes the position of "I am a Man and who is she?! She is some weak, little thing. She needs to be controlled, helped, and taught how to live. I need to take her by the ears and turn her in the direction I want her to go." Then it's not life but mere disrespect coming for that person. Unfortunately, we see this often among couples. It is fantastic when a man and a woman maintain mutual respect and tact. Such couples exist, but sadly, there aren't very many of them.

Often, infidelity takes place in families. The reason for it is the constant search for a vibrant person. Suppose life with your partner is dim and uninteresting. That means something is missing. Why can't we create long-lasting, happy relationships? I mean *truly happy* and not just coexisting, where we tolerate each other, sometimes a little, sometimes a lot, sometimes it's very bad, just like riding a roller coaster.

The Creator built the base for a happy couple. Presume that a man and a woman met and formed a pair. They each have a spiritual foundation, as well as an intellectual one. As a couple, they lived a good life together for some time; however, if they aren't changing spiritually, they start experiencing loss of interest, which is normal. It is laid into the foundation of the human spirit. *The human spirit, by the Law of Evolution, must keep developing.* It must become brighter each day, month after month, and year after year. That applies to both men and women. If such evolution starts taking place, each step in time will yield more vibrant relationships instead of the old ones, which resemble a finished book: "I already know all my wife's habits: what she'll say and how she'll act. It's like telepathy - I know in advance everything about her and vise-versa, nothing new." But our spirit by nature is a wanderer. It is always searching for something new and exciting. That impulse is embedded in us. It is our natural base. Only we don't know how to use it.

Thus, when a man is looking for something more vibrant and finds this body, that body, the third one, the eighths one, the twenty-eighths one, but doesn't get any satisfaction, he eventually turns into a cynic and says, "All women are the same!" A woman with experience says the same thing about men: "You are all the same." In reality, a body will never quench your thirst. Only a soul can do that, and only one that's growing. **Spiritual evolution is the foundation of a happy couple.** Then, if we keep evolving, we continuously experience increased gravitation towards each other. And we will be stunned by the beauty of the relationship that matures, creating a stronger desire to be together. Then this unhealthy, over-stimulated, and inflated sexual interest will decrease. *Joy will arise on the level of the soul, and it will be so powerful that a sexual relationship will pale in comparison.* A sexual relationship is not as important as it has been presented to us.

Another unfortunate trend in family relations is that one thinks their partner owes them something. That kind of mentality leads to one trying to subjugate another to their will. There are "alpha" women or "alpha" men who are overpowering. In reality, we must *respect* each other's interests and tendencies, helping one another on this path. We must become less demanding, *which will show respect for the Law of Freedom of Choice.* It's not only showing respect for your partner or society, but it is, *first and foremost, respect for God's Law.* In my spiritual work, that was my main incentive.

126

So, we must improve our relationship with the opposite sex and learn to respect each other's interests. *If a man and a woman find true love for each other, the Darkness will be defeated by that alone!* Because Love is Christ! He said so Himself, "A new Commandment I give you: Love one another. <u>As I have loved you</u>, so you must love one another. By this everyone will know that <u>you are My disciples if you love one another</u>." (John, 13:34-35). "Whoever does not love does not know God, because <u>God is love</u>." (1 John, 4:8). And Antichrist is Anti-Love. *Our sins are stopping us from loving each other.* While we have those demons clinging onto us, they will always break our connection with the soul, with the spirit.

Spirit is Love. This Love must come to Earth and nourish our bodies, bringing harmony and beauty. Thus, if we don't break through and connect with our spirit, we will never be capable of true Love. *Real* Love does not let demons anywhere near It. We must keep that flame going; then everything will be fine. That we must learn.

27. "LOVE YOUR GOD WITH ALL YOUR HEART AND WITH ALL YOUR SOUL AND WITH ALL YOUR MIND"

The human spirit was granted the ability to create forms. If I create a form of connection with God, I say, "God, I believe in You!", and my faith is genuine. Thus, I am completely open - my brain and all of my cloaks are open. That is, my soul and my spirit are open to Him. I *trust Him* sincerely with all my heart. Only help me! Then help comes. Leaning on this help, I begin climbing the spiritual staircase. It is difficult, and each step requires an effort. And it's not just the climbing. *I must also <u>understand</u> and <u>explain</u> to my brain in earthly concepts why I need it!* Jesus said for a reason, "Love your God with all your <u>heart</u> and with all your <u>soul</u> and with all your <u>mind</u>." *We must understand it <u>on all levels</u> of our being!* If you love *intuitively* but don't understand *logically*, then you have not finished your work. Your brain will always resist until you explain this subject to it and force it to live wisely. Then your "tool" gets rid of the junk. Ideas, which have *misled* it until now, stop blocking it. It is free. Because now it is captivated by *one* idea – Live by the Law, and you can sleep soundly. Your present will fuel your future. The good that you do now will become your tomorrow. You do good tomorrow, so it will be the day after. *It all depends on you.*

God made Laws, but by inhabiting us here, He gave us full freedom. And as I do, so my life will develop. That is, everything depends on me! And we say, "All is the Will of Allah! All is the Will of God!" Correct. In the end – yes. Because His Laws control this world, but we are free here. We are meant to be the "re-transmitters" of Light. We must conduct good things in life. If we don't do this, we don't fulfill our meaning of being. Then the Sword of Justice begins to chastise. We have forgotten the Truth, so we now suffer for this forgetfulness. And no one can say that it's undeserved, at least not the believers.

If a person doesn't believe in God, that is his right. The non-believing materialist says, "There is no God because I cannot touch Him, never knew Him, and cannot see Him! What about the injustice and filth of this world? God couldn't arrange such a world! You say yourself that God is justice!" But when you learn the entire design, it turns out that the world *is* just. *Man, by his freedom of choice, created evil.* Only this behavior is finite, meaning we are being tolerated and given helpers for some time. But if we don't follow the instructions, the result is destruction. *And it is not God who is destroying us, but the very evil we have created.* God simply says, "I remove the brakes, and all your Karma, billions of your sins, will collapse on you because I stopped providing you with the protection of Light. If you don't want to live with the Light, the floodgate opens, and everyone gets their own!" Is God judging us? No! Each one writes their own script throughout their history.

At the last moment, we are offered the chance to reform and to live through *part* of our troubles in humility. And God will remove the rest. He says, "Start coming to Me and the majority of your Karma, maybe 90%, I will destroy if only you eliminate at least part of it *to your full extent!* Understand that if you won't work and remove part of your sins, I *cannot* help you!" It is as if you came to visit someone, made a mess, and wanted the host to clean up after you. The Master of this world is too powerful and will force you to participate in this cleaning. And if you choose not to, you will perish. Such are the harsh Laws of Justice. This scenario is happening now. The floodgate is slowly opening, and all unredeemed sins and responsibilities begin to fall on us. Thus, life becomes dreadful. We are experiencing it even on the national scale. Debauchery creeps in from all directions. People are becoming uncultured, and ideology isn't aimed at purity (conscience and morality) but on debauchery, vulgarity, and deceit. It is all due to laziness – one wishes to possess without earning, which has become an unfortunate trend of our society.

Young people don't want to work or study, but they wish to own the best cars and lead a luxurious lifestyle. Many children are raised with that kind of mentality. And no one explains the moral picture to a child. That first you must become a very wise, educated, and strong person who invests his labor; only then will you receive bounty. The child says, "You are right, dad! One must be an honest, decent, hardworking person. But why do the others have it? I see teenagers driving expensive cars. They did not earn it. At best, it is handed to them by their parents, or, what's even worse, they get themselves into some shady business. Where is the justice?" And dad shrugs his shoulders. What can he say? He, as a teacher, cannot explain it. "You will understand once you grow up." The child grows up and strengthens his negative qualities. Then he is almost impossible to correct. So, he starts going downhill. Then prison begins, where he graduates with higher criminal education and becomes a professional villain or degrades as an individual. He is broken so badly that he is no longer a human. That is how people become totally mutilated.

Well, there is no sense in addressing social issues. I just wanted to give you the underlying reason for our downfall. It is because we don't want to live by the Law. Thus, we have no right to a normal, happy, and creative life in all of its aspects. That is all. The basis has been presented!

Of course, I've described the ultimate degradation by using the example of prison. However, to reverse the overall unhealthy tendency of our society, we must realize that raising an individual starts with the parents. When both parents commit to the road of spiritual evolution, a positive shift starts taking place in families, which will inevitably have a favorable impact on our children. Joy will dominate within our families as well as outside, and our children will start learning from us. Then they will say, "My parents are awesome! Why do I need the streets? I am protected from it by this beauty of relationship. I will never trade it for some counterfeit. I will learn to live the way my parents live, rather than listening to some losers on the streets." So, your child will be protected by this example from any degrading influence.

But when the unrighteous parents lecture their child on morals, he doesn't accept it. He starts rebelling. Usually, he cannot openly rebel due to his financial dependence or other circumstances. So, he starts living a double life by his own principles. Where does he find those principles? He finds them in his leaders. Maybe he sees strong personalities on the streets or somewhere else and starts copying them. A child copies his environment until the age of 14–15. If he doesn't have his own individual core, he might be copying into old age. He will copy this person or that one, but there is nothing of his own originality. He didn't accumulate anything. Or he might read piles of books, different authors, and live the life of a bookworm. Some people live through their favorite TV shows. They have no life of their own; they have traded it. But we must live our own lives, instead of submerging into books and TV shows. It's ok to watch some wholesome shows in moderation, but we must be personally present in this life. There may be some useful things to learn, so you might watch an episode and see how one is punished for their foolishness, hesitation, or weakness. But it's not worthy to watch it all day long. When we start living vicariously through the heroes of our favorite TV series, the tradeoff happens. We are being pumped up with shallow and unhealthy thoughts. It is hollow, blank. For us to become "humans", we must *live* and not just exist. We must become full and active participants of this world.

Of course, I am concerned about what's happening in my country and even around the world. Do I care that people suffer? Yes, I am not an unsympathetic person. But instead of reaching for a sedative, because it hurts me to see people dying from drugs, wars, and other adversities, I don't, because a normal person won't faint from suffering for others. *The best benefit is a good deed.* There is such a notion. It is *constructive* to learn how to free yourself and to pass this learned experience on to others. Then your compassion is real! You *do* something, instead of watching the news and simply getting upset at everything falling apart. Nobody will fix anything! Because one can only fix himself! It is at his disposal. We can sometimes not even correct a psyche of our own child because they also have the freedom of choice. If we realized it late, then it is 50/50 – maybe we can correct it, maybe not.

So, I swallowed these bitter truths and realized that my strength depends on the quality of my connection with the Light. The more Light I gained, the more peace came to me. The only valuable work that can be done now is to pass this experience on to people. That is the experience in applying Christianity *without imposing it*. I have no right to demand anything from you, nor to threaten you, nor to lure you in. I can help you! I have presented the arguments and the facts of life. There are people who have studied the system of religion. They put Christianity to practice and have been moving in this direction for a few years now. They have experienced positive changes in their lives, which proves that true Christianity is alive, and the Laws are working, permeating all aspects of our life without fail. When you learn these Laws *and start living by Them,* you will unite with your soul, and your soul is never mistaken.

I have made my goal to help you connect with your soul and never break that bond again. ***Then, your soul will be your guide on Earth, meaning YOU will be the master of your life.*** For your spirit is your soul and is YOU, whereas your body is merely an instrument for your stay on Earth.

I have two modes of delivery of this subject to the pubic – seminars and school. The seminar merely introduces you to the topic of religion and spiritual evolution. I stopped describing human origins, its birth, and some other details. You can obtain a significant amount of information in the book *In the Light of Truth* on your own. My main objective is to deliver the foundation for your spiritual work – how to combat negative emotions, how to get support on this road, and other nuances that you won't find in the book despite all its grandeur. That's done in the school. And the school is for someone who is already committed to the idea. They are storming the Heavens. When I put them into the state of Connection, I become responsible for them. I have to guard them, especially in the beginning. When the going gets tough, I tell people to contact me, and I will help. We have mutual work then. That is a big difference between the seminars and the school.

Of course, this book is primarily addressed to living souls who have faith and seek a way out of life's dead end. Non-believers are not interested in the topic of religion for the time being. I ask you not to view this text as an imposition of personal opinion, even though it is verified by the personal experience of witnessing positive results. Because each one of us bears personal responsibility for our choices, which shape our own destinies – sowing and reaping. Time will tell who is right.

Life is the best teacher, and we must be able to learn from It, for Life is from God!

EPILOGUE

Today, the human spirit remains in a deep sleep. The majority of the Christians, unfortunately, are spiritually inert. But such spirit that is slumbering peacefully will never see the Luminous Heights, for the flight requires the spirit to grow its wings! Man must exert himself if he wishes to reach the Luminous Heights! Paradise awaits those who strive for It. To strive does not mean to just to think, to plead, and to beg God. To strive means *to act*, to exert yourself to get there! Only when you push yourself to live in accordance with the Law of Motion, thus rejecting your laziness, can the Word come to life within you, enabling you to start your ascent into the World of Pure Spirits, which is your *real home*. But before that can happen, you must shatter all the walls around you, which, after thousands of years, your spiritual laziness has allowed to reach an enormous height and a great width. These walls are what is constricting the wings of your spirit, keeping them frozen in the stage of deadly underdevelopment.

Nevertheless, many people much rather run after hollow and misleading concepts which diminish God's Laws, because the comfort they offer is very alluring to the indolent human spirit. Foreseeing this, Jesus once said, "Enter through the narrow gate. For wide is the gate and broad is the road that leads to destruction, and many enter through it. But small is the gate and narrow the road that leads to life, and only a few find it." (Matthew, 7:13-14). Jesus very well was familiar with such human weakness as spiritual laziness, which Lucifer's flunkies successfully indulge through various notions, including the central principle that Jesus Christ redeemed all sins of the believers with His blood.

Blood sacrifice as redemption was voiced primarily by Paul the apostle, although other apostles have made similar statements. Unfortunately, this version replaced the main essence of Christianity, and the "authoritative" opinion of the apostles became the core dogma for all Christian denominations, which satisfies spiritual laziness. That is how the Darkness residing in the minds of people, who did not yet fully comprehend the essence of the Word of God, introduced a lie at the very source of the Christian religion. *The lie that one becomes free from their sins and is spiritually saved not through a personal victory over sin but by the blood of the innocent Son of God.* Thus, obeying the Commandments is the unnecessary hassle for the already "redeemed and saved." That is the way the present-day Christians lead their lives – they believe and they sin simultaneously, justifying their weakness with the quotes of the apostles, while disregarding the Word of God that is in front of them, given by the Savior, "If you love Me, keep My Commandments." (John, 14:15). ***The notion that we are redeemed of our sins by the "perfect sacrifice" became the screen hiding the real key to freedom and soul salvation.***

For almost twenty centuries, humanity has been walking past Christ's Truth, all the while thinking that we are "saved". The result is apparent in cities and villages, on the streets and in families. It manifests in the form of rivalry and hatred between nations and, most revealing, *in hostility* between the Christian denominations. "By this everyone will know that you are My disciples if you love one another." (John, 13:35).

Why wasn't the strict and straightforward teaching of Christ taken as a foundation for the spiritual development of a Christian? Instead, the opinions of the apostles, influenced by Judaism, were accepted as a core of Christianity. The word of the apostles, who were mere *humans*, was *exalted over* the Word of *God*! Why? There is only one reason: a failure to clearly explain how to obey the Commandments and an inability to understand their true essence. Also, we didn't cultivate the tools to fight the diverse and often cleverly camouflaged manifestations of the Darkness in our minds. For that, we need to learn from the experience of people living by the Commandments — people who took on the difficult task of spreading the Word of God *while living by It*. The apostles did not possess the holiness that was attributed to them on their own. They received their righteous qualities from Jesus Christ, who said, "Freely you have received; freely give." (Matthew, 10:8). "Jesus called His twelve disciples to Him and gave them authority to drive out impure spirits and to heal every disease and sickness." (Matthew, 10:1). Remember that the term "apostle" does not mean "holy." The word "apostle" translates from Greek as "the one who is sent to preach." Satan also has his apostles.

If Christ chose people who came to Him and later became apostles, that means they were deserving, spiritually strong individuals, perhaps the best of their day. The apostles did everything in their *human power*. We owe them for spreading Christianity across the world, thanks to their sacrificial missionary work. It is not the apostles' fault that the interpreters choose to follow their imperfect understanding of the Word, to the detriment of the true Word of the Son of God.

The moan is spreading across the Earth, so where can we find justice? Without accurately understanding the essence of the Christian religion, we stand defenseless before an onslaught of evil. *We refuse to remove the log of sin out of our eye.* Instead, we continuously search for someone to blame for our misfortunes while forgetting the critical and perpetual Law that carves us, the Law that what we sow, so must we reap a hundredfold.

Those who have attempted to live by the Commandments know how tricky and powerful the Darkness is. It approaches a person mainly through their intellect, in the form of thoughts disguised as their own. A follower can be led to the beginning of their spiritual work only through true faith, uncompromising self-control, sincere prayer, resistance to their own *pseudo-thinking*, and the strongest willpower, which must be applied regularly. In addition, willpower must be supported by God's Will, through baptism. The next step is to never relax even for a minute for the rest of your life.

The road to freedom is hard, for we allowed ourselves to be imprisoned by our sins. "Very truly I tell you, everyone who sins is a slave to sin." (John, 8:34). Speaking in simple terms, we are the slaves of envy, resentment, anger, despondency, fear, lust, jealousy, vanity, greed, and so on. These vices shape our external behavior. Each negative emotion *has keys for resisting it*, which we need to learn and internalize.

Let me remind you of several main virtues, without which the movement to the Light remains only an illusion:

1. *Repentance*. "Penitent heads don't get chopped off." (Proverb)

2. *Faith*. Faith must be a genuine, spiritual perception rather than an intellectual statement.

3. *Goal*. The main goal is to free your soul. It must prevail over any earthly goals.

4. Having your *brain under the control of your spirit*, your conscience.

5. Presence of *will*.

6. Presence of *patience*.

7. Presence of *humility*. Possessing real humility means *accepting the right of the Law to return our sins to us in the form of punishment*. If the

acceptance is genuine, then forgiveness is genuine and, thus, the sin is forgiven. That sin is redeemed with pain and loss. "For if you forgive other people when they sin against you, your heavenly Father will also forgive you. But if you do not forgive others their sins, your Father will not forgive your sins." (Matthew, 6:14).

All of the above qualities must manifest in the presence of *real baptism*. Only a priest who possesses spiritual faith is able to baptize. Additionally, the baptized one must understand the essence of baptism. The Holy Spirit protects only those who have real faith. And real faith means openness to God, along with a consistent reduction of personal sins which dirty this world. Otherwise, a person loses support from Above. Remember the warning of the Son of God – Head of the Church, "<u>Not everyone</u> who says to Me: 'Lord, Lord' will enter the Kingdom of Heaven, <u>but only the one who does the will of My Father who is in Heaven</u>." (Matthew, 7:21). *Conforming to the Will of the Father means fulfilling His Commandments.* ***In doing so lies the salvation of the soul from the enslavement of sins.***

Jesus predicted the Second Coming. He knew that humanity would be unable to climb out of the surrounding sea of lies and misfortune without help from Above. But do you think the Second One will bring a new message? Just like the First One, He will proclaim, "If you love Me, keep My Commandments." And if we are incapable of living by the Law of God, which means loving Him, then we will face His Judgement. Or perhaps another apostle will suggest that our sins are redeemed through blood sacrifice? Especially considering all of the many sins we have amassed by now! Except this time, there will be no blood sacrifice because, on the day of His welcoming, all enemies will be preoccupied with saving their own skin, because the Second Messenger, the Spirit of Truth, will come to establish order on Earth. If Christ was Love, the last "physician" visiting Earth, then the Second One is God's Will, "the surgeon" who comes to remove a malignant tumor from the face of the Earth.

There is an interesting quatrain from the 16th century:

"So long-awaited will never return,

Homeland in Europe, he will appear in Asia:

The only one who comes from the league of the great Hermes,

And he will rise above all the Kings of the East."

Nostradamus, (Century 10, Quatrain 75).

How to interpret this quatrain?

It will not be Jesus who comes but Immanuel – the Spirit of Truth, which is another hypostasis of God.

He will be of European descent born in Asia,

The only successor to all God's Messengers.

The Truth that He brings will rise above all branches of religions, including eastern ones.

CHRONOLOGICAL INDEX:

NOTES

NOTES